DAN-16   DANTES SUBJECT STANDARDIZED TESTS (DSST)

This is your
PASSBOOK for...

General Anthropology

Test Preparation Study Guide
Questions & Answers

NATIONAL LEARNING CORPORATION®

COPYRIGHT NOTICE

This book is SOLELY intended for, is sold ONLY to, and its use is RESTRICTED to individual, bona fide applicants or candidates who qualify by virtue of having seriously filed applications for appropriate license, certificate, professional and/or promotional advancement, higher school matriculation, scholarship, or other legitimate requirements of education and/or governmental authorities.

This book is NOT intended for use, class instruction, tutoring, training, duplication, copying, reprinting, excerption, or adaptation, etc., by:

1) Other publishers
2) Proprietors and/or Instructors of "Coaching" and/or Preparatory Courses
3) Personnel and/or Training Divisions of commercial, industrial, and governmental organizations
4) Schools, colleges, or universities and/or their departments and staffs, including teachers and other personnel
5) Testing Agencies or Bureaus
6) Study groups which seek by the purchase of a single volume to copy and/or duplicate and/or adapt this material for use by the group as a whole without having purchased individual volumes for each of the members of the group
7) Et al.

Such persons would be in violation of appropriate Federal and State statutes.

PROVISION OF LICENSING AGREEMENTS – Recognized educational, commercial, industrial, and governmental institutions and organizations, and others legitimately engaged in educational pursuits, including training, testing, and measurement activities, may address request for a licensing agreement to the copyright owners, who will determine whether, and under what conditions, including fees and charges, the materials in this book may be used them. In other words, a licensing facility exists for the legitimate use of the material in this book on other than an individual basis. However, it is asseverated and affirmed here that the material in this book CANNOT be used without the receipt of the express permission of such a licensing agreement from the Publishers. Inquiries re licensing should be addressed to the company, attention rights and permissions department.

All rights reserved, including the right of reproduction in whole or in part, in any form or by any means, electronic or mechanical, including photocopying, recording, or by any information storage and retrieval system, without permission in writing from the Publisher.

Copyright © 2025 by
National Learning Corporation

212 Michael Drive, Syosset, NY 11791
(516) 921-8888 • www.passbooks.com
E-mail: info@passbooks.com

PASSBOOK® SERIES

THE *PASSBOOK® SERIES* has been created to prepare applicants and candidates for the ultimate academic battlefield – the examination room.

At some time in our lives, each and every one of us may be required to take an examination – for validation, matriculation, admission, qualification, registration, certification, or licensure.

Based on the assumption that every applicant or candidate has met the basic formal educational standards, has taken the required number of courses, and read the necessary texts, the *PASSBOOK® SERIES* furnishes the one special preparation which may assure passing with confidence, instead of failing with insecurity. Examination questions – together with answers – are furnished as the basic vehicle for study so that the mysteries of the examination and its compounding difficulties may be eliminated or diminished by a sure method.

This book is meant to help you pass your examination provided that you qualify and are serious in your objective.

The entire field is reviewed through the huge store of content information which is succinctly presented through a provocative and challenging approach – the question-and-answer method.

A climate of success is established by furnishing the correct answers at the end of each test.

You soon learn to recognize types of questions, forms of questions, and patterns of questioning. You may even begin to anticipate expected outcomes.

You perceive that many questions are repeated or adapted so that you can gain acute insights, which may enable you to score many sure points.

You learn how to confront new questions, or types of questions, and to attack them confidently and work out the correct answers.

You note objectives and emphases, and recognize pitfalls and dangers, so that you may make positive educational adjustments.

Moreover, you are kept fully informed in relation to new concepts, methods, practices, and directions in the field.

You discover that you are actually taking the examination all the time: you are preparing for the examination by "taking" an examination, not by reading extraneous and/or supererogatory textbooks.

In short, this PASSBOOK®, used directedly, should be an important factor in helping you to pass your test.

NONTRADITIONAL EDUCATION

Students returning to school as adults bring more varied experience to their studies than do the teenagers who begin college shortly after graduating from high school. As a result, there are numerous programs for students with nontraditional learning curves. Hundreds of colleges and universities grant degrees to people who cannot attend classes at a regular campus or have already learned what the college is supposed to teach.

You can earn nontraditional education credits in many ways:
- Passing standardized exams
- Demonstrating knowledge gained through experience
- Completing campus-based coursework, and
- Taking courses off campus

Some methods of assessing learning for credit are objective, such as standardized tests. Others are more subjective, such as a review of life experiences.

With some help from four hypothetical characters – Alice, Vin, Lynette, and Jorge – this article describes nontraditional ways of earning educational credit. It begins by describing programs in which you can earn a high school diploma without spending 4 years in a classroom. The college picture is more complicated, so it is presented in two parts: one on gaining credit for what you know through course work or experience, and a second on college degree programs. The final section lists resources for locating more information.

Earning High School Credit

People who were prevented from finishing high school as teenagers have several options if they want to do so as adults. Some major cities have back-to-school programs that allow adults to attend high school classes with current students. But the more practical alternatives for most adults are to take the General Educational Development (GED) tests or to earn a high school diploma by demonstrating their skills or taking correspondence classes.

Of course, these options do not match the experience of staying in high school and graduating with one's friends. But they are viable alternatives for adult learners committed to meeting and, often, continuing their educational goals.

GED Program

Alice quit high school her sophomore year and took a job to help support herself, her younger brother, and their newly widowed mother. Now an adult, she wants to earn her high school diploma – and then go on to college. Because her job as head cook and her family responsibilities keep her busy during the day, she plans to get a high school equivalency diploma. She will study for, and take, the GED tests. Every year, about half a million adults earn their high school credentials this way. A GED diploma is accepted in lieu of a high school one by more than 90 percent of employers, colleges, and universities, so it is a good choice for someone like Alice.

The GED testing program is sponsored by the American Council on Education and State and local education departments. It consists of examinations in five subject areas: Writing, science, mathematics, social studies, and literature and the arts. The tests also measure skills such as analytical ability, problem solving, reading comprehension, and ability to understand and apply information. Most of the questions are multiple choice; the writing test includes an essay section on a topic of general interest.

Eligibility rules for taking the exams vary, but some states require that you must be at least 18. Tests are given in English, Spanish, and French. In addition to standard print, versions in large print, Braille, and audiocassette are also available. Total time allotted for the tests is 7 1/2 hours.

The GED tests are not easy. About one-fourth of those who complete the exams every year do not pass. Passing scores are established by administering the tests to a sample of graduating high school seniors. The minimum standard score is set so that about one-third of graduating seniors would not pass the tests if they took them.

Because of the difficulty of the tests, people need to prepare themselves to take them. Often, they start by taking the Official GED Practice Tests, usually available through a local adult education center. Centers are listed in your phone book's blue pages under "Adult Education," "Continuing Education," or "GED." Adult education centers also have information about GED preparation classes and self-study materials. Classes are generally arranged to accommodate adults' work schedules. National Learning Corporation publishes several study guides that aim to thoroughly prepare test-takers for the GED.

School districts, colleges, adult education centers, and community organizations have information about GED testing schedules and practice tests. For more information, contact them, your nearest GED testing center, or:

GED Testing Service
One Dupont Circle, NW, Suite 250
Washington, DC 20036-1163
1(800) 62-MY GED (626-9433)
(202) 939-9490

Skills Demonstration

Adults who have acquired high school level skills through experience might be eligible for the National External Diploma Program. This alternative to the GED does not involve any direct instruction. Instead, adults seeking a high school diploma must demonstrate mastery of 65 competencies in 8 general areas: Communication; computation; occupational preparedness; and self, social, consumer, scientific, and technological awareness.

Mastery is shown through the completion of the tasks. For example, a participant could prove competency in computation by measuring a room for carpeting, figuring out the amount of carpet needed, and computing the cost.

Before being accepted for the program, adults undergo an evaluation. Tests taken at one of the program's offices measure reading, writing, and mathematics abilities. A take-home segment includes a self-assessment of current skills, an individual skill evaluation, and an occupational interest and aptitude test.

Adults accepted for the program have weekly meetings with an assessor. At the meeting, the assessor reviews the participant's work from the previous week. If the task has not been completed properly, the assessor explains the mistake. Participants continue to correct their errors until they master each competency. A high school diploma is awarded upon proven mastery of all 65 competencies.

Fourteen States and the District of Columbia now offer the External Diploma Program. For more information, contact:

External Diploma Program
One Dupont Circle, NW, Suite 250
Washington, DC 20036-1193
(202) 939-9475

Correspondence and Distance Study

Vin dropped out of high school during his junior year because his family's frequent moves made it difficult for him to continue his studies. He promised himself at the time he dropped out that he would someday finish the courses needed for his diploma. For people like Vin, who prefer to earn a traditional diploma in a nontraditional way, there are about a dozen accredited courses of study for earning a high school diploma by correspondence, or distance study. The programs are either privately run, affiliated with a university, or administered by a State education department.

Distance study diploma programs have no residency requirements, allowing students to continue their studies from almost any location. Depending on the course of study, students need not be enrolled full time and usually have more flexible schedules for finishing their work. Selection of courses ranges from vo-tech to college prep, and some programs place different emphasis on the types of diplomas offered. University affiliated schools, for example, allow qualified students to take college courses along with their high school ones. Students can then apply the college credits toward a degree at that university or transfer them to another institution.

Taking courses by distance study is often more challenging and time consuming than attending classes, especially for adults who have other obligations. Success depends on each student's motivation. Students usually do reading assignments on their own. Written exercises, which they complete and send to an instructor for grading, supplement their reading material.

A list of some accredited high schools that offer diplomas by distance study is available free from the Distance Education and Training Council, formerly known as the National Home Study Council. Request the "DETC Directory of Accredited Institutions" from:

The Distance Education and Training Council
1601 18th Street, NW.
Washington, DC 20009-2529
(202) 234-5100

Some publications profiling nontraditional college programs include addresses and descriptions of several high school correspondence ones. See the Resources section at the end of this article for more information.

Getting College Credit For What You Know

Adults can receive college credit for prior coursework, by passing examinations, and documenting experiential learning. With help from a college advisor, nontraditional students should assess their skills, establish their educational goals, and determine the number of college credits they might be eligible for.

Even before you meet with a college advisor, you should collect all your school and training records. Then, make a list of all knowledge and abilities acquired through experience, no matter how irrelevant they seem to your chosen field. Next, determine your educational goals: What specific field do you wish to study? What kind of a degree do you want? Finally, determine how your past work fits into the field of study. Later on, you will evaluate educational programs to find one that's right for you.

People who have complex educational or experiential learning histories might want to have their learning evaluated by the Regents Credit Bank. The Credit Bank, operated by Regents College of the University of the State of New York, allows people to consolidate credits earned through college, experience, or other methods. Special assessments are available for Regents College enrollees whose knowledge in a specific field cannot be adequately evaluated by standardized exams. For more information, contact the Regents Credit Bank at:

Regents College
7 Columbia Circle
Albany, NY 12203-5159
(518) 464-8500

Credit For Prior College Coursework

When Lynette was in college during the 1970s, she attended several different schools and took a variety of courses. She did well in some classes and poorly in others. Now that she is a successful business owner and has more focus, Lynette thinks she should forget about her previous coursework and start from scratch. Instead, she should start from where she is.

Lynette should have all her transcripts sent to the colleges or universities of her choice and let an admissions officer determine which classes are applicable toward a degree. A few credits here and there may not seem like much, but they add up. Even if the subjects do not seem relevant to any major, they might be counted as elective credits toward a degree. And comparing the cost of transcripts with the cost of college courses, it makes sense to spend a few dollars per transcript for a chance to save hundreds, and perhaps thousands, of dollars in books and tuition.

Rules for transferring credits apply to all prior coursework at accredited colleges and universities, whether done on campus or off. Courses completed off campus, often called extended learning, include those available to students through independent study and correspondence. Many schools have extended learning programs; Brigham Young University, for example, offers more than 300 courses through its Department of Independent Study. One type of extended learning is distance learning, a form of correspondence study by technological means such as television, video and audio, CD-ROM, electronic mail, and computer tutorials. See the Resources section at the end of this article for more information about publications available from the National University Continuing Education Association.

Any previously earned college credits should be considered for transfer, no matter what the subject or the grade received. Many schools do not accept the transfer of courses graded below a C or ones taken more than a designated number of years ago. Some colleges and universities also have limits on the number of credits that can be transferred and applied toward a degree. But not all do. For example, Thomas Edison State College, New Jersey's State college for adults, accepts the transfer of all 120 hours of credit required for a baccalaureate degree – provided all the credits are transferred from regionally accredited schools, no more than 80 are at the junior college level, and the student's grades overall and in the field of study average out to C.

To assign credit for prior coursework, most schools require original transcripts. This means you must complete a form or send a written, signed request to have your transcripts released directly to a college or university. Once you have chosen the schools you want to apply to, contact the schools you attended before. Find out how much each transcript costs, and ask them to send your transcripts to the ones you are applying to. Write a letter that includes your name (and names used during attendance, if different) and dates of attendance, along with the names and addresses of the schools to which your transcripts should be sent. Include payment and mail to the registrar at the schools you have attended. The registrar's office will process your request and send an official transcript of your coursework to the colleges or universities you have designated.

Credit For Noncollege Courses

Colleges and universities are not the only ones that offer classes. Volunteer organizations and employers often provide formal training worth college credit. The American Council on Education has two programs that assess thousands of specific courses and make recommendations on the amount of college credit they are worth. Colleges and universities accept the recommendations or use them as guidelines.

One program evaluates educational courses sponsored by government agencies, business and industry, labor unions, and professional and voluntary organizations. It is the Program on Noncollegiate Sponsored Instruction (PONSI). Some of the training seminars Alice has participated in covered topics such as food preparation, kitchen safety, and nutrition. Although she has not yet earned her GED, Alice can earn college credit because of her completion of these formal job-training seminars. The number of credits each seminar is worth does not hinge on Alice's current eligibility for college enrollment.

The other program evaluates courses offered by the Army, Navy, Air Force, Marines, Coast Guard, and Department of Defense. It is the Military Evaluations Program. Jorge has never attended college, but the engineering technology classes he completed as part of his military training are worth college credit. And as an Army veteran, Jorge is eligible for a service that takes the evaluations one step further. The Army/American Council on Education Registry Transcript System (AARTS) will provide Jorge with an individualized transcript of American Council on Education credit recommendations for all courses he completed, the military occupational specialties (MOS's) he held, and examinations he passed while in the Army. All Army and National Guard enlisted personnel and veterans who enlisted after October 1981 are eligible for the transcript. Similar services are being considered by the Navy and Marine Corps.

To obtain a free transcript, see your Army Education Center for a 5454R transcript request form. Include your name, Social Security number, basic active service date, and complete address where you want the transcript sent. Mail your request to:

AARTS Operations Center
415 McPherson Ave.
Fort Leavenworth, KS 66027-1373

Recommendations for PONSI are published in *The National Guide to Educational Credit for Training Programs;* military program recommendations are in *The Guide to the Evaluation of Educational Experiences in the Armed Forces.* See the Resources section at the end of this article for more information about these publications.

Former military personnel who took a foreign language course through the Defense Language Institute may request course transcripts by sending their name, Social Security number, course title, duration of the course, and graduation date to:

Commandant, Defense Language Institute
Attn: ATFL-DAA-AR
Transcripts
Presidio of Monterey
Monterey, CA 93944-5006

Not all of Jorge's and Alice's courses have been assessed by the American Council on Education. Training courses that have no Council credit recommendation should still be assessed by an advisor at the schools they want to attend. Course descriptions, class notes, test scores, and other documentation may be helpful for comparing training courses to their college equivalents. An oral examination or other demonstration of competency might also be required.

There is no guarantee you will receive all the credits you are seeking – but you certainly won't if you make no attempt.

Credit By Examination

Standardized tests are the best-known method of receiving college credit without taking courses. These exams are often taken by high school students seeking advanced placement for college, but they are also available to adult learners. Testing programs and colleges and universities offer exams in a number of subjects. Two U.S. Government institutes have foreign language exams for employees that also may be worth college credit.

It is important to understand that receiving a passing score on these exams does not mean you get college credit automatically. Each school determines which test results it will accept, minimum scores required, how scores are converted for credit, and the amount of credit, if any, to be assigned. Most colleges and universities accept the American Council on Education credit recommendations, published every other year in the 250-page *Guide to Educational Credit by Examination*. For more information, contact:

The American Council on Education
Credit by Examination Program
One Dupont Circle, Suite 250
Washington, DC 20036-1193
(202) 939-9434

Testing programs:

You might know some of the five national testing programs by their acronyms or initials: CLEP, ACT PEP: RCE, DANTES, AP, and NOCTI. (The meanings of these initialisms are explained below.) There is some overlap among programs; for example, four of them have introductory accounting exams. Since you will not be awarded credit more than once for a specific subject, you should carefully evaluate each program for the subject exams you wish to take. And before taking an exam, make sure you will be awarded credit by the college or university you plan to attend.

CLEP (College-Level Examination Program), administered by the College Board, is the most widely accepted of the national testing programs; more than 2,800 accredited schools award credit for passing exam scores. Each test covers material taught in basic undergraduate courses. There are five general exams – English composition, humanities, college mathematics, natural sciences, and social sciences and history – and many subject exams. Most exams are entirely multiple-choice, but English composition exams may include an essay section. For more information, contact:

CLEP
P.O. Box 6600
Princeton, NJ 08541-6600
(609) 771-7865

ACT PEP: RCE (American College Testing Proficiency Exam Program: Regents College Examinations) tests are given in 38 subjects within arts and sciences, business, education, and nursing. Each exam is recommended for either lower- or upper-level credit. Exams contain either objective or extended response questions, and are graded according to a standard score, letter grade, or pass/fail. Fees vary, depending on the subject and type of exam. For more information or to request free study guides, contact:

ACT PEP: Regents College Examinations
P.O. Box 4014
Iowa City, IA 52243
(319) 337-1387
(New York State residents must contact Regents College directly.)

DANTES (Defense Activity for Nontraditional Education Support) standardized tests are developed by the Educational Testing Service for the Department of Defense. Originally administered only to military personnel, the exams have been available to the public since 1983. About 50 subject tests cover business, mathematics, social science, physical science, humanities, foreign languages, and applied technology. Most of the tests consist entirely of multiple-choice questions. Schools determine their own administering fees and testing schedules. For more information or to request free study sheets, contact:

DANTES Program Office
Mail Stop 31-X
Educational Testing Service
Princeton, NJ 08541
1(800) 257-9484

The AP (Advanced Placement) Program is a cooperative effort between secondary schools and colleges and universities. AP exams are developed each year by committees of college and high school faculty appointed by the College Board and assisted by consultants from the Educational Testing Service. Subjects include arts and languages, natural sciences, computer science, social sciences, history, and mathematics. Most tests are 2 or 3 hours long and include both multiple-choice and essay questions. AP courses are available to help students prepare for exams, which are offered in the spring. For more information about the Advanced Placement Program, contact:

Advanced Placement Services
P.O. Box 6671
Princeton, NJ 08541-6671
(609) 771-7300

NOCTI (National Occupational Competency Testing Institute) assessments are designed for people like Alice, who have vocational-technical skills that cannot be evaluated by other tests. NOCTI assesses competency at two levels: Student/job ready and teacher/experienced worker. Standardized evaluations are available for occupations such as auto-body repair, electronics, mechanical drafting, quantity food preparation, and upholstering. The tests consist of multiple-choice questions and a performance component. Other services include workshops, customized assessments, and pre-testing. For more information, contact:

NOCTI
500 N. Bronson Ave.
Ferris State University
Big Rapids, MI 49307
(616) 796-4699

Colleges and universities:

Many colleges and universities have credit-by-exam programs, through which students earn credit by passing a comprehensive exam for a course offered by the institution. Among the most widely recognized are the programs at Ohio University, the University of North Carolina, Thomas Edison State College, and New York University.

Ohio University offers about 150 examinations for credit. In addition, you may sometimes arrange to take special examinations in non-laboratory courses offered at Ohio University. To take a test for credit, you must enroll in the course. If you plan to transfer the credit earned, you also need written permission from an official at your school. Books and study materials are available, for a cost, through the university. Exams must be taken within 6 months of the enrollment date; most last 3 hours. You may arrange to take the exam off campus if you do not live near the university.

Ohio University is on the quarter-hour system; most courses are worth 4 quarter hours, the equivalent of 3 semester hours. For more information, contact:

Independent Study
Tupper Hall 302
Ohio University
Athens, OH 45701-2979
1(800) 444-2910
(614) 593-2910

The University of North Carolina offers a credit-by-examination option for 140 independent study (correspondence) courses in foreign languages, humanities, social sciences, mathematics, business administration, education, electrical and computer engineering, health administration, and natural sciences. To take an exam, you must request and receive approval from both the course instructor and the independent studies department. Exams must be taken within six months of enrollment, and you may register for no more than two at a time. If you are not near the University's Chapel Hill campus, you may take your exam under supervision at an accredited college, university, community college, or technical institute. For more information, contact:

Independent Studies
CB #1020, The Friday Center
UNC-Chapel Hill
Chapel Hill, NC 27599-1020
1(800) 862-5669 / (919) 962-1134

The Thomas Edison College Examination Program offers more than 50 exams in liberal arts, business, and professional areas. Thomas Edison State College administers tests twice a month in Trenton, New Jersey; however, students may arrange to take their tests with a proctor at any accredited American college or university or U.S. military base. Most of the tests are multiple choice; some also include short answer or essay questions. Time limits range from 90 minutes to 4 hours, depending on the exam. For more information, contact:

Thomas Edison State College
TECEP, Office of Testing and Assessment
101 W. State Street
Trenton, NJ 08608-1176
(609) 633-2844

New York University's Foreign Language Program offers proficiency exams in more than 40 languages, from Albanian to Yiddish. Two exams are available in each language: The 12-point test is equivalent to 4 undergraduate semesters, and the 16-point exam may lead to upper level credit. The tests are given at the university's Foreign Language Department throughout the year.

Proof of foreign language proficiency does not guarantee college credit. Some colleges and universities accept transcripts only for languages commonly taught, such as French and Spanish. Nontraditional programs are more likely than traditional ones to grant credit for proficiency in other languages.

For an informational brochure and registration form for NYU's foreign language proficiency exams, contact:

New York University
Foreign Language Department
48 Cooper Square, Room 107
New York, NY 10003
(212) 998-7030

Government institutes:

The Defense Language Institute and Foreign Service Institute administer foreign language proficiency exams for personnel stationed abroad. Usually, the tests are given at the end of intensive language courses or upon completion of service overseas. But some people – like Jorge, who knows Spanish – speak another language fluently and may be allowed to take a proficiency exam in that language before completing their tour of duty. Contact one of the offices listed below to obtain transcripts of those scores. Proof of proficiency does not guarantee college credit, however, as discussed above.

To request score reports from the Defense Language Institute for Defense Language Proficiency Tests, send your name, Social Security number, language for which you were tested, and, most importantly, when and where you took the exam to:

Commandant, Defense Language Institute
Attn: ATFL-ES-T
DLPT Score Report Request
Presidio of Monterey
Monterey, CA 93944-5006

To request transcripts of scores for Foreign Service Institute exams, send your name, Social Security number, language for which you were tested, and dates or year of exams to:

Foreign Service Institute
Arlington Hall
4020 Arlington Boulevard
Rosslyn, VA 22204-1500
Attn: Testing Office (Send your request to the attention of the testing office of the foreign language in which you were tested)

Credit For Experience

Experiential learning credit may be given for knowledge gained through job responsibilities, personal hobbies, volunteer opportunities, homemaking, and other experiences. Colleges and universities base credit awards on the knowledge you have attained, not for the experience alone. In addition, the knowledge must be college level; not just any learning will do. Throwing horseshoes as a hobby is not likely to be worth college credit. But if you've done research on how and where the sport originated, visited blacksmiths, organized tournaments, and written a column for a trade journal – well, that's a horseshoe of a different color.

Adults attempting to get credit for their experience should be forewarned: Having your experience evaluated for college credit is time-consuming, tedious work – not an easy shortcut for people who want quick-fix college credits. And not all experience, no matter how valuable, is the equivalent of college courses.

Requesting college credit for your experiential learning can be tricky. You should get assistance from a credit evaluations officer at the school you plan to attend, but you should also have a general idea of what your knowledge is worth. A common method for converting knowledge into credit is to use a college catalog. Find course titles and descriptions that match what you have learned through experience, and request the number of credits offered for those courses.

Once you know what credit to ask for, you must usually present your case in writing to officials at the college you plan to attend. The most common form of presenting experiential learning for credit is the portfolio. A portfolio is a written record of your knowledge along with a request for equivalent college credit. It includes an identification and description of the knowledge for which you are requesting credit, an explanatory essay of how the knowledge was gained and how it fits into your educational plans, documentation that you have acquired such knowledge, and a request for college credit. Required elements of a portfolio vary by schools but generally follow those guidelines.

In identifying knowledge you have gained, be specific about exactly what you have learned. For example, it is not enough for Lynette to say she runs a business. She must identify the knowledge she has gained from running it, such as personnel management, tax law, marketing strategy, and inventory review. She must also include brief descriptions about her knowledge of each to support her claims of having those skills.

The essay gives you a chance to relay something about who you are. It should address your educational goals, include relevant autobiographical details, and be well organized, neat, and convey confidence. In his essay, Jorge might first state his goal of becoming an engineer. Then he would explain why he joined the Army, where he got hands-on training and experience in developing and servicing electronic equipment.

This, he would say, led to his hobby of creating remote-controlled model cars, of which he has built 20. His conclusion would highlight his accomplishments and tie them to his desire to become an electronic engineer.

Documentation is evidence that you've learned what you claim to have learned. You can show proof of knowledge in a variety of ways, including audio or video recordings, letters from current or former employers describing your specific duties and job performance, blueprints, photographs or artwork, and transcripts of certifying exams for professional licenses and certification – such as Alice's certification from the American Culinary Federation. Although documentation can take many forms, written proof alone is not always enough. If it is impossible to document your knowledge in writing, find out if your experiential learning can be assessed through supplemental oral exams by a faculty expert.

Earning a College Degree

Nontraditional students often have work, family, and financial obligations that prevent them from quitting their jobs to attend school full time. Can they still meet their educational goals? Yes.

More than 150 accredited colleges and universities have nontraditional bachelor's degree programs that require students to spend little or no time on campus; over 300 others have nontraditional campus-based degree programs. Some of those schools, as well as most junior and community colleges, offer associate's degrees nontraditionally. Each school with a nontraditional course of study determines its own rules for awarding credit for prior coursework, exams, or experience, as discussed previously. Most have charges on top of tuition for providing these special services.

Several publications profile nontraditional degree programs; see the Resources section at the end of this article for more information. To determine which school best fits your academic profile and educational goals, first list your criteria. Then, evaluate nontraditional programs based on their accreditation, features, residency requirements, and expenses. Once you have chosen several schools to explore further, write to them for more information. Detailed explanations of school policies should help you decide which ones you want to apply to.

Get beyond the printed word – especially the glowing words each school writes about itself. Check out the schools you are considering with higher education authorities, alumni, employers, family members, and friends. If possible, visit the campus to talk to students and instructors and sit in on a few classes, even if you will be completing most or all of your work off campus. Ask school officials questions about such things as enrollment numbers, graduation rate, faculty qualifications, and confusing details about the application process or academic policies. After you have thoroughly investigated each prospective college or university, you can make an informed decision about which is right for you.

Accreditation

Accreditation is a process colleges and universities submit to voluntarily for getting their credentials. An accredited school has been investigated and visited by teams of observers and has periodic inspections by a private accrediting agency. The initial review can take two years or more.

Regional agencies accredit entire schools, and professional agencies accredit either specialized schools or departments within schools. Although there are no national accrediting standards, not just any accreditation will do. Countless "accreditation associations" have been invented by schools, many of which have no academic programs and sell phony degrees, to accredit themselves. But 6 regional and about 80 professional accrediting associations in the United States are recognized by the U.S. Department of Education or the Commission on Recognition of Postsecondary Accreditation. When checking accreditation, these are the names to look for. For more information about accreditation and accrediting agencies, contact:

> Institutional Participation Oversight Service Accreditation and State Liaison Division
> U.S. Department of Education
> ROB 3, Room 3915
> 600 Independence Ave., SW
> Washington, DC 20202-5244
> (202) 708-7417

Because accreditation is not mandatory, lack of accreditation does not necessarily mean a school or program is bad. Some schools choose not to apply for accreditation, are in the process of applying, or have educational methods too unconventional for an accrediting association's standards. For the nontraditional student, however, earning a degree from a college or university with recognized accreditation is an especially important consideration. Although nontraditional education is becoming more widely accepted, it is not yet mainstream. Employers skeptical of a degree earned in a nontraditional manner are likely to be even less accepting of one from an unaccredited school.

Program Features

Because nontraditional students have diverse educational objectives, nontraditional schools are diverse in what they offer. Some programs are geared toward helping students organize their scattered educational credits to get a degree as quickly as possible. Others cater to those who may have specific credits or experience but need assistance in completing requirements. Whatever your educational profile, you should look for a program that works with you in obtaining your educational goals.

A few nontraditional programs have special admissions policies for adult learners like Alice, who plan to earn their GEDs but want to enroll in college in the meantime. Other features of nontraditional programs include individualized learning agreements, intensive academic counseling, cooperative learning and internship placement, and waiver of some prerequisites or other requirements – as well as college credit for prior coursework, examinations, and experiential learning, all discussed previously.

Lynette, whose primary goal is to finish her degree, wants to earn maximum credits for her business experience. She will look for programs that do not limit the number of credits awarded for equivalency exams and experiential learning. And since well-documented proof of knowledge is essential for earning experiential learning credits, Lynette should make sure the program she chooses provides assistance to students submitting a portfolio.

Jorge, on the other hand, has more credits than he needs in certain areas and is willing to forego some. To become an engineer, he must have a bachelor's degree; but because he is accustomed to hands-on learning, Jorge is interested in getting experience as he gains more technical skills. He will concentrate on finding schools with strong cooperative education, supervised fieldwork, or internship programs.

Residency Requirements

Programs are sometimes deemed nontraditional because of their residency requirements. Many people think of residency for colleges and universities in terms of tuition, with in-state students paying less than out-of-state ones. Residency also may refer to where a student lives, either on or off campus, while attending school.

But in nontraditional education, residency usually refers to how much time students must spend on campus, regardless of whether they attend classes there. In some nontraditional programs, students need not ever step foot on campus. Others require only a very short residency, such as one day or a few weeks. Many schools have standard residency requirements of several semesters but schedule classes for evenings or weekends to accommodate working adults.

Lynette, who previously took courses by independent study, prefers to earn credits by distance study. She will focus on schools that have no residency requirement. Several colleges and universities have nonresident degree completion programs for adults with some college credit. Under the direction of a faculty advisor, students devise a plan for earning their remaining credits. Methods for earning credits include independent study, distance learning, seminars, supervised fieldwork, and group study at arranged sites. Students may have to earn a certain number of credits through the degree-granting institution. But many programs allow students to take courses at accredited schools of their choice for transfer toward their degree.

Alice wants to attend lectures but has an unpredictable schedule. Her best course of action will be to seek out short residency programs that require students to attend seminars once or twice a semester. She can take courses that are televised and videotape them to watch when her schedule permits, with the seminars helping to ensure that she properly completes her coursework. Many colleges and universities with short residency requirements also permit students to earn some credits elsewhere, by whatever means the student chooses.

Some fields of study require classroom instruction. As Jorge will discover, few colleges and universities allow students to earn a bachelor's degree in engineering entirely through independent study. Nontraditional residency programs are designed to accommodate adults' daytime work schedules. Jorge should look for programs offering evening, weekend, summer, and accelerated courses.

Tuition and Other Expenses

The final decisions about which schools Alice, Jorge, and Lynette attend may hinge in large part on a single issue: Cost. And rising tuition is only part of the equation. Beginning with application fees and continuing through graduation fees, college expenses add up.

Traditional and nontraditional students have some expenses in common, such as the cost of books and other materials. Tuition might even be the same for some courses, especially for colleges and universities offering standard ones at unusual times. But for nontraditional programs, students may also pay fees for services such as credit or transcript review, evaluation, advisement, and portfolio assessment.

Students are also responsible for postage and handling or setup expenses for independent study courses, as well as for all examination and transcript fees for transferring credits. Usually, the more nontraditional the program, the more detailed the fees. Some schools charge a yearly enrollment fee rather than tuition for degree completion candidates who want their files to remain active.

Although tuition and fees might seem expensive, most educators tell you not to let money come between you and your educational goals. Talk to someone in the financial aid department of the school you plan to attend or check your library for publications about financial aid sources. The U.S. Department of Education publishes a guide to Federal aid programs such as Pell Grants, student loans, and work-study. To order the free 74-page booklet, *The Student Guide: Financial Aid from the U.S. Department of Education,* contact:

Federal Student Aid Information Center
P.O. Box 84
Washington, DC 20044
1 (800) 4FED-AID (433-3243)

Resources

Information on how to earn a high school diploma or college degree without following the usual routes is available from several organizations and in numerous publications. Information on nontraditional graduate degree programs, available for master's through doctoral level, though not discussed in this article, can usually be obtained from the same resources that detail bachelor's degree programs.

National Learning Corporation publishes study guides for all of these exams, for both general examinations and tests in specific subject areas. To order study guides, or to browse their catalog featuring more than 5,000 titles, visit NLC online at www.passbooks.com, or contact them by phone at (800) 632-8888.

Organizations

Adult learners should always contact their local school system, community college, or university to learn about programs that are readily available. The following national organizations can also supply information:

American Council on Education
One Dupont Circle
Washington, DC 20036-1193
(202) 939-9300

Within the American Council on Education, the Center for Adult Learning and Educational Credentials administers the National External Diploma Program, the GED Program, the Program on Noncollegiate Sponsored Instruction, the Credit by Examination Program, and the Military Evaluations Program.

DANTES Subject Standardized Tests

INTRODUCTION

The DANTES (Defense Activity for Non-Traditional Education Support) subject standardized tests are comprehensive college and graduate level examinations given by the Armed Forces, colleges and graduate schools as end-of-subject course evaluation final examinations or to obtain college equivalency credits in the various subject areas tested.

The DANTES Examination Program enables students to obtain college credit for what they have learned on the job, through self-study, personal interest, correspondence courses or by any other means. It is used by colleges and universities to award college credit to students who demonstrate that they know as much as students completing an equivalent college course. It is a cost-efficient, time-saving way for students to use their knowledge to accomplish their educational goals.

Most schools accept the American Council on Education (ACE) recommendations for the minimum score required and the amount of credit awarded, but not all schools do. Be sure to check the policy regarding the score level required for credit and the number of credits to be awarded.

Not all tests are accepted by all institutions. Even when a test is accepted by an institution, it may not be acceptable for every program at that institution. Before considering testing, ascertain the acceptability of a specific test for a particular course.

Colleges and universities that administer DANTES tests may administer them to any applicant – or they may administer the tests only to students registered at their institution. Decisions about who will be allowed to test are made by the school. Students should contact the test center to determine current policies and schedules for DANTES testing.

Colleges and universities authorized to administer DANTES tests usually do so throughout the calendar year. Each school sets its own fee for test administration and establishes its own testing schedule. Contact the representative at the administering school directly to make arrangements for testing.

Checklist For Students

✓ Visit **www.getcollegecredit.com** to obtain a list of tests, fact sheets, test preparation materials, participating colleges and universities, and much more.

✓ Contact your school advisor to confirm that the DSST you selected will fit into your curriculum.

✓ Consult the *DSST Candidate Information Bulletin* for answers to specific questions.

✓ Contact the test site to schedule your test.

✓ Prepare for your examination by using the fact sheet as a guide.

✓ Take the test.

If you would like a score report sent to your college or university, it is a good idea to bring the four-digit code with you. You must write the DSST Test Center Code for that institution on your answer sheet at the time of testing. DSST Test Center Codes are noted in the DSST Participating Colleges and Universities listing on the Web site.

If you prefer to send a score report to an institution at a later date, there is a transcript fee of $20 for each transcript ordered.

Thomson Prometric
DSST Program
2000 Lenox Drive, Third Floor
Lawrenceville, NJ 08648

Toll-free: 877-471-9860
609-895-5011

E-mail: pnj-dsst@thomson.com

MAKING A COLLEGE DEGREE WITHIN YOUR REACH

Today, there are many educational alternatives to the classroom—you can learn from your job, your reading, your independent study, and special interests you pursue. You may already have learned the subject matter covered by some college-level courses.

The DSST Program is a nationally recognized testing program that gives you the opportunity to receive college credit for learning acquired outside the traditional college classroom. Colleges and universities throughout the United States administer the program, developed by Thomson Prometric, year-round. Annually, over 90,000 DSSTs are administered to individuals who are interested in continuing their education. Take advantage of the DSST testing program; it speeds the educational process and provides the flexibility adults need, making earning a degree more feasible.

Since requirements differ from college to college, please check with the credit-awarding institution before taking a DSST. More than 1,800 colleges and universities currently award credit for DSSTs, and the number is growing every day. You can choose from 37 test titles in the areas of Social Science, Business, Mathematics, Applied Technology, Humanities, and Physical Science. A brief description of each examination is found on the pages that follow.

Reach Your Career Goals Through DSSTs

Use DSSTs to help you earn your degree, get a promotion, or simply demonstrate that you have college-level knowledge in subjects relevant to your work.

Save Time...

You don't have to sit through classes when you have previously acquired the knowledge or experience for most of what is being taught and can learn the rest yourself. You might be able to bypass introductory-level courses in subject areas you already know.

Save Money...

DSSTs save you money because the classes you bypass by earning credit through the DSST Program are classes you won't have to pay for on your way to earning your degree. You can use the money instead to take more advanced courses that can be more challenging and rewarding.

Improve Your Chances for Admission to College

Each college has its own admission policies; however, having passing scores for DSSTs on your transcript can provide strong evidence of how well you can perform at the college level.

Gain Confidence Performing at a College Level

Many adults returning to college find that lack of confidence is often the greatest hurdle to overcome. Passing a DSST demonstrates your ability to perform on a college level.

Make Up for Courses You May Have Missed

You may be ready to graduate from college and find that you are a few credits short of earning your degree. By using semester breaks, vacation time, or leisure time to study independently, you can prepare to take one or more DSSTs, fulfill your academic requirements, and graduate on time.

If You Cannot Attend Regularly Scheduled Classes...

If your lifestyle or responsibilities prevent you from attending regularly scheduled classes, you can earn your college degree from a college offering an external degree program. The DSST Program allows you to earn your degree by study and experience outside the traditional classroom.

Many colleges and universities offer external degree or distance learning programs. For additional information, contact the college you plan to attend or:

Center for Lifelong Learning
American Council on Education
One DuPont Circle NW, Suite 250
Washington, DC 20036
202-939-9475
www.acenet.edu
(Select "Center for Lifelong Learning" under "Programs & Services"
for more information)

Fact Sheets

For each test, there is a Fact Sheet that outlines the topics covered by each test and includes a list of sample questions, a list of recommended references of books that would be useful for review, and the number of credits awarded for a passing score as recommended by the American Council on Education (ACE). *Please note that some schools require scores that are higher than the minimum ACE-recommended passing score.* It is suggested that you check with your college or university to determine what score they require in order to earn credit. You can obtain Fact Sheets by:
- Downloading them from www.getcollegecredit.com
- E-mailing a request to pnj-dsst@thomson.com
- Completing a Candidate Publications Order Form

DSST Online Practice Tests

DSST online practice tests contain items that reflect a *partial range of difficulty* identified in the Content Outline section on each Fact Sheet. There is an online DSST Practice Test in the following categories:
- Mathematics
- Social Science
- Business
- Physical Science
- Applied Technology
- Humanities

Although the online DSST Practice Test questions do not indicate the full range of difficulty you would find in an actual DSST test, they will help you assess your knowledge level. Each online DSST Practice Test can be purchased by visiting www.getcollegecredit.com and clicking on DSST Practice Exams.

TAKING DSST EXAMINATIONS

Earning College Credit for DSST Examinations

To find out if the college of your choice awards credit for passing DSST scores, contact the admissions office or counseling and testing office. The college can also provide information on the scores required for awarding credit, the number of credit hours awarded, and any courses that can be bypassed with satisfactory scores.

It is important that you contact the institution of your choice as early as possible since credit-awarding policies differ among colleges and universities.

Where to Take DSSTs

DSSTs are administered at colleges and universities nationwide. Each location determines the frequency and scheduling of test administrations. To obtain the most current list of participating DSST colleges and universities:
- Visit and download the information from www.getcollegecredit.com
- E-mail pnj-dsst@thomson.com

Scheduling Your Examination

Please be aware that some colleges and universities provide DSST testing services to enrolled students only. After you have selected a college or university that administers DSSTs, you will need to contact them to schedule your test date.

The fee to take a DSST is $60 per test. This fee entitles you to two score reports after the test is scored. One will be sent directly to you and the other will be sent to the college or university that you designate on your answer sheet. You may pay the test fee with a certified check or U.S. money order made payable to Thomson Prometric or you may charge the test fee to your Visa, MasterCard or American Express credit card. Note: The credit card statement will reflect a charge from Thomson Prometric for all DSST examinations. *(Declined credit card charges will be assessed an additional $25 processing fee.)*

In addition, the test site may also require a test administration fee for each examination, to be paid directly to the institution. Contact the test site to determine its administration fee and payment policy.

Other Testing Arrangements

If you are unable to find a participating DSST college or university in your area, you may want to contact the testing office of a local accredited college or university to determine whether a representative from that office will agree to administer the test(s) for you.

The school's representative should then contact the DSST Program at 866-794-3497 to arrange for this administration. If you are unable to locate a test site, contact Thomson Prometric for assistance at pnj-dsst@thomson.com or 866-794-3497.

Testing Accommodations for Students with Disabilities

Thomson Prometric is committed to serving test takers with disabilities by providing services and reasonable testing accommodations as set forth in the provisions of the *Americans with Disabilities Act* (ADA). If you have a disability, as prescribed by the ADA, and require special testing services or arrangements, please contact the test administrator at the test site. You will be asked to submit to the test administrator documentation of your disability and your request for special accommodations. The test administrator will then forward your documentation along with your request for testing accommodations to Thomson Prometric for approval.

Please submit your request as far in advance of your test date as possible so that the necessary accommodations can be made. Only test takers with documented disabilities are eligible for special accommodations.

On the Day of the Examination

It is important to review this information and to have the correct identification present on the day of the examination:

- Arrive on time as a courtesy to the test administrator.
- Bring a valid form of government-issued identification that includes a current photo and your signature (acceptable documents include a driver's license, passport, state-issued identification card or military identification). *Anyone who fails to present valid identification will not be allowed to test.*
- Bring several No. 2 (soft-lead) sharpened pencils with good erasers, a watch, and a black pen if you will be writing an essay.
- Do not bring books or papers.
- Do not bring an alarm watch that beeps, a telephone, or a phone beeper into the testing room.
- The use of nonprogrammable calculators, slide rules, scratch paper and/or other materials is permitted for some of the tests.

DSST SCORING POLICIES

Your DSST examination scores are reported only to you, unless you request that they be sent elsewhere. If you want your scores sent to your college, you must provide the correct DSST code number of the school on your answer sheet at the time you take the test. See the *DSST Directory of Colleges and Universities* on the Web site www.getcollegecredit.com.

If your institution is not listed, contact Thomson Prometric at 866-794-3497 to establish a code number. (Some schools may require a student to be enrolled prior to receiving a score report.)

Receiving Your Score Report

Allow approximately four weeks after testing to receive your score report.

Calling DSST Customer Service before the required four-week score processing time has elapsed will not expedite the processing of your scores. Due to privacy and security requirements, scores will not be reported to students over the telephone under any circumstance.

Scoring of Principles of Public Speaking Speeches

The speech portion of the *Principles of Public Speaking* examination will be sent to speech raters who are faculty members at accredited colleges that currently teach or have previously taught the course. Scores for the *Principles of Public Speaking* examination are available six to eight weeks from receipt by Thomson Prometric. If you take the *Principles of Public Speaking* examination and fail (either the objective, speech portion, or both), you must follow the retesting policy waiting period of six months (180 days) before retaking the entire exam.

Essays

The essays for *Ethics in America* and *Technical Writing* are <u>optional</u> and thus are not scored by raters. The essays are forwarded to the college or university that you designate, along with your score report, for their use in determining the award of credit. <u>Before taking the *Ethics in America* or *Technical Writing* examinations, check with your college or university to determine whether the essay is required.</u>

NOTE: *Principles of Public Speaking* speech topic cassette tapes and essays are kept on file at Thomson Prometric for one year from the date of administration.

How to Get Transcripts

There is a $20 fee for each transcript you request. Payment must be in the form of a certified check, U.S. money order payable to Thomson Prometric, or credit card. Personal checks and debit cards are NOT an acceptable method of payment. One transcript may include scores for one or more examinations taken. To request a transcript, download the Transcript Order Form from www.getcollegecredit.com.

DESCRIPTION OF THE DSST EXAMINATIONS

Mathematics

- **Fundamentals of College Algebra** covers mathematical concepts such as fundamental algebraic operations; linear, absolute value; quadratic equations, inequalities, radials, exponents and logarithms, factoring polynomials and graphing. The use of a nonprogrammable, handheld calculator is permitted.

- **Principles of Statistics** tests the understanding of the various topics of statistics, both qualitatively and quantitatively, and the ability to apply statistical methods to solve a variety of problems. The topics included in this test are descriptive statistics; correlation and regression; probability; chance models and sampling and tests of significance. The use of a nonprogrammable, handheld calculator is permitted.

Social Science

- **Art of the Western World** deals with the history of art during the following periods: classical; Romanesque and Gothic; early Renaissance; high Renaissance, Baroque; rococo; neoclassicism and romanticism; realism, impressionism and post-impressionism; early twentieth century; and post-World War II.

- **Western Europe Since 1945** tests the knowledge of basic facts and terms and the understanding of concepts and principles related to the areas of the historical background of the aftermath of the Second World War and rebuilding of Europe; national political systems; issues and policies in Western European societies; European institutions and processes; and Europe's relations with the rest of the world.

- **An Introduction to the Modern Middle East** emphasizes core knowledge (including geography, Judaism, Christianity, Islam, ethnicity); nineteenth-century European impact; twentieth-century Western influences; World Wars I and II; new nations; social and cultural changes (1900-1960) and the Middle East from 1960 to present.

- **Human/Cultural Geography** includes the Earth and basic facts (coordinate systems, maps, physiography, atmosphere, soils and vegetation, water); culture and environment, spatial processes (social processes, modern economic systems, settlement patterns, political geography); and regional geography.

- **Rise and Fall of the Soviet Union** covers Russia under the Old Regime; the Revolutionary Period; New Economic Policy; Pre-war Stalinism; The Second World War; Post-war Stalinism; The Khrushchev Years; The Brezhnev Era; and reform and collapse.

- **A History of the Vietnam War** covers the history of the roots of the Vietnam War; the First Vietnam War (1946-1954); pre-war developments (1954-1963); American involvement in the Vietnam War; Tet (1968); Vietnamizing the War (1968-1973); Cambodia and Laos; peace; legacies and lessons.

- **The Civil War and Reconstruction** covers the Civil War from presecession (1861) through Reconstruction. It includes causes of the war; secession; Fort Sumter; the war in the east and in the west; major battles; the political situation; assassination of Lincoln; end of the Confederacy; and Reconstruction.

- **Foundations of Education** includes topics such as contemporary issues in education; past and current influences on education (philosophies, democratic ideals, social/economic influences); and the interrelationships between contemporary issues and influences.

- **Life-span Developmental Psychology** covers models and theories; methods of study; ethical issues; biological development; perception, learning and memory; cognition and language; social, emotional, and personality development; social behaviors, family life cycle, extrafamilial settings; singlehood and cohabitation; occupational development and retirement; adjustment to life stresses; and bereavement and loss.

- **Drug and Alcohol Abuse** includes such topics as drug use in society; classification of drugs; pharmacological principles; alcohol (types, effects of, alcoholism); general principles and use of sedative hypnotics, narcotic analgesics, stimulants, and hallucinogens; other drugs (inhalants, steroids); and prevention/treatment.

- **General Anthropology** deals with anthropology as a discipline; theoretical perspectives; physical anthropology; archaeology; social organization; economic organization; political organization; religion; and modernization and application of anthropology.

- **Introduction to Law Enforcement** includes topics such as history and professional movement of law enforcement; overview of the U.S. criminal justice system; police systems in the U.S.; police organization, management, and issues; and U.S. law and precedents.

- **Criminal Justice** deals with criminal behavior (crime in the U.S., theories of crime, types of crime); the criminal justice system (historical origins, legal foundations, due process); police; the court system (history and organization, adult court system, juvenile court, pre-trial and post-trial processes); and corrections.

- **Fundamentals of Counseling** covers historical development (significant influences and people); counselor roles and functions; the counseling relationship; and theoretical approaches to counseling.

Business
- **Principles of Finance** deals with financial statements and planning; time value of money; working capital management; valuation and characteristics; capital budgeting; cost of capital; risk and return; and international financial management. The use of a nonprogrammable, handheld calculator is permitted.

- **Principles of Financial Accounting** includes topics such as general concepts and principles, accounting cycle and classification; transaction analysis; accruals and deferrals; cash and internal control; current accounts; long- and short-term liabilities; capital stock; and financial statements. The use of a nonprogrammable, handheld calculator is permitted.

- **Human Resource Management** covers general employment issues; job analysis; training and development; performance appraisals; compensation issues; security issues; personnel legislation and regulation; labor relations and current issues; an overview of the Human Resource Management Field; Human Resource Planning; Staffing; training and development; compensation issues; safety and health; employee rights and discipline; employment law; labor relations and current issues and trends.

- **Organizational Behavior** deals with the study of organizational behavior (scientific approaches, research designs, data collection methods); individual processes and characteristics; interpersonal and group processes and characteristics; organizational processes and characteristics; and change and development processes.

- **Principles of Supervision** deals with the roles and responsibilities of the supervisor; management functions (planning, organization and staffing, directing at the supervisory level); and other topics (legal issues, stress management, union environments, quality concerns).

- **Business Law II** covers topics such as sales of goods; debtor and creditor relations; business organizations; property; and commercial paper.

- **Introduction to Computing** includes topics such as history and technological generations; hardware/software; applications to information technology; program development; data management; communications and connectivity; and computing and society. The use of a nonprogrammable, handheld calculator is permitted.

- **Management Information Systems** covers systems theory, analysis and design of systems, hardware and software; database management; telecommunications; management of the MIS functional area and informational support.

- **Introduction to Business** deals with economic issues affecting business; international business; government and business; forms of business ownership; small business, entrepreneurship and franchise; management process; human resource management; production and operations; marketing management; financial management; risk management and insurance; and management and information systems.

- **Money and Banking** covers the role and kinds of money; commercial banks and other financial intermediaries; central banking and the Federal Reserve system; money and macroeconomics activity; monetary policy in the U.S.; and the international monetary system.

- **Personal Finance** includes topics such as financial goals and values; budgeting; credit and debt; major purchases; taxes; insurance; investments; and retirement and estate planning. The use of auxiliary materials, such as calculators and slide rules, is NOT permitted.

- **Business Mathematics** deals with basic operations with integers, fractions, and decimals; round numbers; ratios; averages; business graphs; simple interest; compound interest and annuities; net pay and deductions; discounts and markups; depreciation and net worth; corporate securities; distribution of ownership; and stock and asset turnover.

Physical Science
• **Astronomy** covers the history of astronomy, celestial mechanics; celestial systems; astronomical instruments; the solar system; nature and evolution; the galaxy; the universe; determining astronomical distances; and life in the universe.

• **Here's to Your Health** covers mental health and behavior; human development and relationships; substance abuse; fitness and nutrition; risk factors, disease, and disease prevention; and safety, consumer awareness, and environmental concerns.

• **Environment and Humanity** deals with topics such as ecological concepts (ecosystems, global ecology, food chains and webs); environmental impacts; environmental management and conservation; and political processes and the future.

• **Principles of Physical Science I** includes physics: Newton's Laws of Motion; energy and momentum; thermodynamics; wave and optics; electricity and magnetism; chemistry: properties of matter; atomic theory and structure; and chemical reactions.

• **Physical Geology** covers Earth materials; igneous, sedimentary, and metamorphic rocks; surface processes (weathering, groundwater, glaciers, oceanic systems, deserts and winds, hydrologic cycle); internal Earth processes; and applications (mineral and energy resources, environmental geology).

Applied Technology
• **Technical Writing** covers topics such as theory and practice of technical writing; purpose, content, and organizational patterns of common types of technical documents; elements of various technical reports; and technical editing. Students have the option to write a short essay on one of the technical topics provided. Thomson Prometric will not score the essay; however, for determining the award of credit, a copy of the essay will be forwarded to the college or university you've designated along with the score report or transcript.

Humanities
• **Ethics in America** deals with ethical traditions (Greek views, Biblical traditions, moral law, consequential ethics, feminist ethics); ethical analysis of issues arising in interpersonal and personal-societal relationships and in professional and occupational roles; and relationships between ethical traditions and the ethical analysis of situations. Students have the option to write an essay to analyze a morally problematic situation in terms of issues relevant to a decision and arguments for alternative positions. Thomson Prometric will not score the essay; however, for determining the award of credit, a copy of the essay will be forwarded to the college or university you've designated along with the score report or transcript.

• **Introduction to World Religions** covers topics such as dimensions and approaches to religion; primal religions; Hinduism; Buddhism; Confucianism; Taoism; Judaism; Christianity; and Islam.

• **Principles of Public Speaking** consists of two parts: Part One consists of multiple-choice questions covering considerations of Principles of Public Speaking; audience analysis; purposes of speeches; structure/organization; content/supporting materials; research; language and style; delivery; communication apprehension; listening and feedback; and criticism and evaluation. Part Two requires the student to record an impromptu persuasive speech that will be scored.

FREQUENTLY ASKED QUESTIONS ABOUT DSSTs

In order to pass the test, must I study from one of the recommended references?

The recommended references are a listing of books that were being used as textbooks in college courses of the same or similar title at the time the test was developed. Appropriate textbooks for study are not limited to those listed in the fact sheet. If you wish to obtain study resources to prepare for the examination, you may reference either the current edition of the listed titles or textbooks currently used at a local college or university for the same class title. It is recommended that you reference more than one textbook on the topics outlined in the fact sheet. You should begin by checking textbook content against the content outline included on the front page of the DSST fact sheet before selecting textbooks that cover the text content from which to study. Textbooks may be found at the campus bookstore of a local college or university offering a course on the subject.

Is there a penalty for guessing on the tests?

There is no penalty for guessing on DSSTs, so you should mark an answer for each question.

How much time will I have to complete the test?

Many DSSTs can be completed within 90 minutes; however, additional time can be allowed if necessary.

What should I do if I find a test question irregularity?

Continue testing and then report the irregularity to the test administrator after the test. This may be done by asking that the test administrator note the irregularity on the Supervisor's Irregularity Report or you can write to Thomson Prometric, DSST Program, 2000 Lenox Drive, Third Floor, Lawrenceville, NJ 08648, and indicate the form and question number(s) or circumstances as well as your name and address.

When will I receive my score report?

Allow approximately four weeks from the date of testing to receive your score report. Allow six to eight weeks to receive a score report for the *Principles of Public Speaking* examination.

Will my test scores be released without my permission?

Your test score will not be released to anyone other than the school you designate on your answer sheet unless you write to us and ask us to send a transcript elsewhere. Instructions about how to do this can be found on your score report. Your scores may be used for research purposes, but individual scores are never made public nor are individuals identified if research findings are made public.

If I do not achieve a passing score on the test, how long must I wait until I can take the test again?

If you do not receive a score on the test that will enable you to obtain credit for the course, you may take the test again after six months (180 days). Please do not attempt to take the test before six months (180 days) have passed because you will receive a score report marked *invalid* and your test fee will not be refunded.

Can my test scores be canceled?

The test administrator is required to report any irregularities to Thomson Prometric. <u>The consequence of bringing unauthorized materials into the testing room, or giving or receiving help, will be the forfeiture of your test fee and the invalidation of test scores.</u> The DSST Program reserves the right to cancel scores and not issue score reports in such situations.

What can I do if I feel that my test scores were not accurately reported?

Thomson Prometric recognizes the extreme importance of test results to candidates and has a multi-step quality-control procedure to help ensure that reported scores are accurate. If you have reason to believe that your score(s) were not accurately reported, you may request to have your answer sheet reviewed and hand scored.

The fees for this service are:
- $20 fee if requested within six months of the test date
- $30 fee if requested more than six months from the test date
- $30 fee if a re-evaluation of the *Principles of Public Speaking* speech is requested

The fee for this service can be paid by credit card or by certified check or U.S. money order payable to Thomson Prometric. Submit your request for score verification along with the appropriate fee or credit card information (credit card number and expiration date) to Thomson Prometric, DSST Program, 2000 Lenox Drive, Third Floor, Lawrenceville, NJ 08648. Include your full name, the test title, the date you took the test, and your Social Security number. Candidates will be notified if a scoring discrepancy is discovered within four weeks of receipt of the request.

What does ACE recommendation mean?

The ACE recommendation is the minimum passing score recommended by the American Council on Education for any given test. It is equivalent to the average score of students in the DSST norming sample who received a grade of C for the course. Some schools require a score higher than the ACE recommendation.

Who is NLC?

National Learning Corporation (NLC) has been successfully preparing candidates for 40 years for over 5,000 exams. NLC publishes Passbook® study guides to help candidates prepare for all DANTES and CLEP exams and almost every other type of exam from high school through adult career.

Go to our website — <u>www.passbooks.com</u> — or call (800) 632-8888 for information about ordering our Passbooks.

To get detailed information on the DSST program and DSST preparation materials, visit <u>www.getcollegecredit.com</u>.

If you are interested in taking the DSST exams, call 877-471-9860 or e-mail <u>pnj-dsst@thomson.com</u>.

DSST EXAM CONTENT FACT SHEET

DSST® GENERAL ANTHROPOLOGY

EXAM INFORMATION

This exam was developed to enable schools to award credit to students for knowledge equivalent to that learned by students taking the course. This exam deals with theoretical perspectives; physical anthropology; archaeology; social organization; economic organization; political organization; religion; and modernization and application of anthropology.

The exam contains 100 questions to be answered in 2 hours.

EXAM CONTENT OUTLINE

The following is an outline of the content areas covered in the examination. The approximate percentage of the examination devoted to each content area is also noted.

I. **Anthropology as a Discipline Branches and Methodologies – 7%**
   a. Physical anthropology
   b. Cultural Anthropology: ethnology; ethnography
   c. Linguistics
   d. Archaeology

II. **Various Theoretical Perspectives – 3%**
   a. Structuralism
   b. Functionalism
   c. Cultural ecology
   d. Cultural evolution
   e. Cultural determinism

III. **Physical Anthropology – 17%**
   a. Genetic principles: genes, heredity, Mendelian inheritance, genotypes
   b. Phenotypes, gene pools, mutations, molecular genetics
   c. Adaptation, natural selection, variations (e.g., blood chemistry)
   d. Living primates
   e. Fossils
      1. Relative and absolute dating
      2. Fossil hominids – A*ustralophithecines, Homo erectus, Homo habilis, Homo sapiens (neanderthalensis* and *sapiens*)

IV. **Archaeology – 19%**
   a. Methodology (prehistoric and historic)
   b. Paleolithic and Mesolithic
   c. Neolithic: development of technology, domestication of plants and animals
   d. Development of civilization and urban societies

V. **Nature of Culture – 12%**
   a. Symbols and symbolic systems
   b. Language, sociolinguistics, morphology, phonology
   c. Society vs. culture
   d. Cultural variation: universals and alternatives
   e. Real vs. ideal culture
   f. Cultural change: invention, diffusion, innovation
   g. Cultural relativity, ethnocentrism
   h. Etic and emic world views
   i. The individual in culture
   j. The arts

VI. **Social Organization – 16%**
   a. Marriage and family patterns: mate choice, residence, monogamy, polygamy, family of orientation – conjugal, natal family, incest, exogamy, divorce
   b. Kinship and descent groups: kindred, lineage, clan, phraty, moiety, bilateral vs. unilateral descent, matrilineal, patrilineal, kinship terminology
   c. Groups and associations (e.g., age, sex)
   d. Social stratification: caste, class, slavery, status (achieved and ascribed), role, rank

VII. **Economic Organization – 7%**
   a. Subsistence and settlement patterns
   b. Formal and substantive approaches
   c. Communal and private ownership of land, material and nonmaterial property
   d. Reciprocity, redistribution, and market exchange
   e. Production, allocation, use, and consumption of goods and services

VIII. **Political Organization – 6%**
   a. Politics, political systems: bands, tribes, states, chiefdoms
   b. Political associations
   c. Social control: customs, laws, war

IX. **Religion – 10%**
   a. Religious institutions (e.g. individual, shamanistic, revitalization movements)
   b. Belief systems, world views (e.g., animism, totemism, myth)
   c. Religious practices and practitioners (e.g. magic, healers)
   d. Rites of passage: birth, maturity, marriage, death

For educational purposes from the official announcement

X. **Modernization and Application of Anthropology – 3%**
   a. Applied anthropology
   b. Cultural survival
   c. Directed cultural change

REFERENCES

Below is a list of reference publications that were either used as a reference to create the exam, or were used as textbooks in college courses of the same or similar title at the time the test was developed. You may reference either the current edition of these titles **or** textbooks currently used at a local college or university for the same class title. It is recommended that you reference **more than one textbook** on the topics outlined in this fact sheet.

You should **begin by checking textbook content against the content outline** provided **before** selecting textbooks that cover the test content from which to study.

Sources for study material are suggested but not limited to the following:

1. Barrett, Richard A. *Culture and Conduct: An Excursion in Anthropology.* Belmont, CA: Wadsworth Publishing, current edition.
2. Fagin, Brian. *People of the Earth: An Introduction to World Prehistory.* Glenview, IL: Scott, Foresman & Co., current edition.
3. Ember, Carol R. and Melvin Ember. *Anthropology.* Englewood Cliffs, NJ: Prentice-Hall, current edition.
4. Harris, Marvin. *Cultural Anthropology.* New York: Harper and Row, current edition.
5. Haviland, William A. *Anthropology.* New York: Holt, Rinehart and Winston, current edition.
6. Jolly, Clifford and Fred Plog. *Physical Anthropology and Archaeology.* New York: Knopf, current edition.
7. Kottak, Conrad P. *Anthropology: The Exploration of Human Diversity.* New York: Random House, current edition.
8. Nanda, Serena. *Cultural Anthropology.* Belmont, CA: Wadsworth Publishing, current edition.
9. Rosman, Abraham and Paula Rubel. *Tapestry of Culture.* New York: Random House, current edition.
10. Sharer, Robert and Wendy Ashmore. *Archaeology: Discovering Our Past.* Palo Alto, CA: Mayfield, current edition.
11. Swartz, Mark J. and David K. Jordan. *Culture: The Anthropological Perspective.* New York: John Wiley, current edition.
12. Thomas, D.H. *Archaeology.* New York: Holt, Rinehart and Winston, current edition.

SAMPLE QUESTIONS

All test questions are in a multiple-choice format, with one correct answer and three incorrect options. These are samples of the types of questions that may appear on the exam. Other sample questions can be found in the form of practice exams by visiting our website at **www.getcollegecredit.com/testprep**.

---

1. Which of the following statements best describes the concept of culture?
   a. Culture consists of genetically transmitted patterns of thinking and acting.
   b. Culture represents economic and political achievements.
   c. Culture is primarily determined by artifacts and art.
   d. Culture consists of learned and shared patterns of thinking and acting.

2. A major contribution by Darwin is the
   a. Principle of uniformism
   b. Theory of diffusionism
   c. Theory of organic solidarity
   d. Theory of natural selection

3. All of the following have traditionally been advanced as possible reasons for the incest taboo EXCEPT the
   a. Necessity to create alliances with other groups
   b. Instinctual sexual aversion to relatives
   c. Deleterious effects of continued inbreeding
   d. Example set by nonhuman primates

4. The Mesolithic era is often described as a period of transition because it
   a. Allowed for the development of great hunting cultures
   b. Is characterized as a period of major growth in the early cities
   c. Witnessed a sharp decline in the development of tools
   d. Represented a period of diversification of subsistence strategies

5. Which of the following statements about ideal cultural patterns (norms) is true?
   a. There is often great discrepancy between what people say they do and what they actually do.

b. A norm ceases to exist if the normative rule is not carried out in social behavior.
c. Norms are seldom outmoded or maladaptive.
d. Ideal cultural patterns are found only among peoples who practice agriculture.

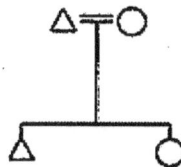

6. The diagram above shows
   a. An extended family
   b. A patrilineage
   c. A nuclear family
   d. A matrifocal family

7. Which of the following is true of traits of humans and not true of other animals?
   a. Prolonged care of young
   b. Sedentary residence patterns
   c. Complex symbol systems
   d. Socialization of young

8. Jane Goodall observed chimpanzees in the wild and was surprised to find that they
   a. Lived in large groups
   b. Made and used tools
   c. Lived in nuclear families
   d. Used sign language

9. The careful description of a culture is called
   a. Epistemology
   b. Phenomenology
   c. Ethnography
   d. Ethnomethodology

10. The special norm that a person must marry someone who is within his or her group is called
    a. Endogamy
    b. Group marriage
    c. Exogamy
    d. Polyandry

CREDIT RECOMMENDATIONS

The American Council on Education's College Credit Recommendation Service (ACE CREDIT) has evaluated the DSST test development process and content of this exam. It has made the following recommendations:

Area or Course Equivalent	General Anthropology
Level	Lower-level baccalaureate
Amount of Credit	Three (3) semester hours
Minimum Score	400
Source	American Council on Education – College Credit Recommendation Service

Answers to sample questions: 1-D; 2-D; 3-D; 4-D; 5-A; 6-C; 7-C; 8-B; 9-C; 10-A.

HOW TO TAKE A TEST

You have studied long, hard and conscientiously.

With your official admission card in hand, and your heart pounding, you have been admitted to the examination room.

You note that there are several hundred other applicants in the examination room waiting to take the same test.

They all appear to be equally well prepared.

You know that nothing but your best effort will suffice. The "moment of truth" is at hand: you now have to demonstrate objectively, in writing, your knowledge of content and your understanding of subject matter.

You are fighting the most important battle of your life—to pass and/or score high on an examination which will determine your career and provide the economic basis for your livelihood.

What extra, special things should you know and should you do in taking the examination?

I. YOU MUST PASS AN EXAMINATION

A. WHAT EVERY CANDIDATE SHOULD KNOW
Examination applicants often ask us for help in preparing for the written test. What can I study in advance? What kinds of questions will be asked? How will the test be given? How will the papers be graded?

B. HOW ARE EXAMS DEVELOPED?
Examinations are carefully written by trained technicians who are specialists in the field known as "psychological measurement," in consultation with recognized authorities in the field of work that the test will cover. These experts recommend the subject matter areas or skills to be tested; only those knowledges or skills important to your success on the job are included. The most reliable books and source materials available are used as references. Together, the experts and technicians judge the difficulty level of the questions.
Test technicians know how to phrase questions so that the problem is clearly stated. Their ethics do not permit "trick" or "catch" questions. Questions may have been tried out on sample groups, or subjected to statistical analysis, to determine their usefulness.
Written tests are often used in combination with performance tests, ratings of training and experience, and oral interviews. All of these measures combine to form the best-known means of finding the right person for the right job.

II. HOW TO PASS THE WRITTEN TEST

A. BASIC STEPS

1) Study the announcement

How, then, can you know what subjects to study? Our best answer is: "Learn as much as possible about the class of positions for which you've applied." The exam will test the knowledge, skills and abilities needed to do the work.

Your most valuable source of information about the position you want is the official exam announcement. This announcement lists the training and experience qualifications. Check these standards and apply only if you come reasonably close to meeting them. Many jurisdictions preview the written test in the exam announcement by including a section called "Knowledge and Abilities Required," "Scope of the Examination," or some similar heading. Here you will find out specifically what fields will be tested.

2) Choose appropriate study materials

If the position for which you are applying is technical or advanced, you will read more advanced, specialized material. If you are already familiar with the basic principles of your field, elementary textbooks would waste your time. Concentrate on advanced textbooks and technical periodicals. Think through the concepts and review difficult problems in your field.

These are all general sources. You can get more ideas on your own initiative, following these leads. For example, training manuals and publications of the government agency which employs workers in your field can be useful, particularly for technical and professional positions. A letter or visit to the government department involved may result in more specific study suggestions, and certainly will provide you with a more definite idea of the exact nature of the position you are seeking.

3) Study this book!

III. KINDS OF TESTS

Tests are used for purposes other than measuring knowledge and ability to perform specified duties. For some positions, it is equally important to test ability to make adjustments to new situations or to profit from training. In others, basic mental abilities not dependent on information are essential. Questions which test these things may not appear as pertinent to the duties of the position as those which test for knowledge and information. Yet they are often highly important parts of a fair examination. For very general questions, it is almost impossible to help you direct your study efforts. What we can do is to point out some of the more common of these general abilities needed in public service positions and describe some typical questions.

1) General information

Broad, general information has been found useful for predicting job success in some kinds of work. This is tested in a variety of ways, from vocabulary lists to questions about current events. Basic background in some field of work, such as sociology or economics, may be sampled in a group of questions. Often these are principles which have become familiar to most persons through exposure rather than through formal training. It is difficult to advise you how to study for these questions; being alert to the world around you is our best suggestion.

2) Verbal ability

An example of an ability needed in many positions is verbal or language ability. Verbal ability is, in brief, the ability to use and understand words. Vocabulary and grammar tests are typical measures of this ability. Reading comprehension or paragraph interpretation questions are common in many kinds of civil service tests. You are given a paragraph of written material and asked to find its central meaning.

IV. KINDS OF QUESTIONS

1. Multiple-choice Questions

Most popular of the short-answer questions is the "multiple choice" or "best answer" question. It can be used, for example, to test for factual knowledge, ability to solve problems or judgment in meeting situations found at work.

A multiple-choice question is normally one of three types:
- It can begin with an incomplete statement followed by several possible endings. You are to find the one ending which best completes the statement, although some of the others may not be entirely wrong.
- It can also be a complete statement in the form of a question which is answered by choosing one of the statements listed.
- It can be in the form of a problem – again you select the best answer.

Here is an example of a multiple-choice question with a discussion which should give you some clues as to the method for choosing the right answer:

When an employee has a complaint about his assignment, the action which will best help him overcome his difficulty is to
    A. discuss his difficulty with his coworkers
    B. take the problem to the head of the organization
    C. take the problem to the person who gave him the assignment
    D. say nothing to anyone about his complaint

In answering this question, you should study each of the choices to find which is best. Consider choice "A" – Certainly an employee may discuss his complaint with fellow employees, but no change or improvement can result, and the complaint remains unresolved. Choice "B" is a poor choice since the head of the organization probably does not know what assignment you have been given, and taking your problem to him is known as "going over the head" of the supervisor. The supervisor, or person who made the assignment, is the person who can clarify it or correct any injustice. Choice "C" is, therefore, correct. To say nothing, as in choice "D," is unwise. Supervisors have and interest in knowing the problems employees are facing, and the employee is seeking a solution to his problem.

2. True/False

3. Matching Questions

Matching an answer from a column of choices within another column.

V. RECORDING YOUR ANSWERS

Computer terminals are used more and more today for many different kinds of exams.

For an examination with very few applicants, you may be told to record your answers in the test booklet itself. Separate answer sheets are much more common. If this separate answer sheet is to be scored by machine – and this is often the case – it is highly important that you mark your answers correctly in order to get credit.

VI. BEFORE THE TEST

YOUR PHYSICAL CONDITION IS IMPORTANT

If you are not well, you can't do your best work on tests. If you are half asleep, you can't do your best either. Here are some tips:

1) Get about the same amount of sleep you usually get. Don't stay up all night before the test, either partying or worrying—DON'T DO IT!
2) If you wear glasses, be sure to wear them when you go to take the test. This goes for hearing aids, too.
3) If you have any physical problems that may keep you from doing your best, be sure to tell the person giving the test. If you are sick or in poor health, you relay cannot do your best on any test. You can always come back and take the test some other time.

Common sense will help you find procedures to follow to get ready for an examination. Too many of us, however, overlook these sensible measures. Indeed, nervousness and fatigue have been found to be the most serious reasons why applicants fail to do their best on civil service tests. Here is a list of reminders:

- Begin your preparation early – Don't wait until the last minute to go scurrying around for books and materials or to find out what the position is all about.
- Prepare continuously – An hour a night for a week is better than an all-night cram session. This has been definitely established. What is more, a night a week for a month will return better dividends than crowding your study into a shorter period of time.
- Locate the place of the exam – You have been sent a notice telling you when and where to report for the examination. If the location is in a different town or otherwise unfamiliar to you, it would be well to inquire the best route and learn something about the building.
- Relax the night before the test – Allow your mind to rest. Do not study at all that night. Plan some mild recreation or diversion; then go to bed early and get a good night's sleep.
- Get up early enough to make a leisurely trip to the place for the test – This way unforeseen events, traffic snarls, unfamiliar buildings, etc. will not upset you.
- Dress comfortably – A written test is not a fashion show. You will be known by number and not by name, so wear something comfortable.
- Leave excess paraphernalia at home – Shopping bags and odd bundles will get in your way. You need bring only the items mentioned in the official notice you received; usually everything you need is provided. Do not bring reference books to the exam. They will only confuse those last minutes and be taken away from you when in the test room.

- Arrive somewhat ahead of time – If because of transportation schedules you must get there very early, bring a newspaper or magazine to take your mind off yourself while waiting.
- Locate the examination room – When you have found the proper room, you will be directed to the seat or part of the room where you will sit. Sometimes you are given a sheet of instructions to read while you are waiting. Do not fill out any forms until you are told to do so; just read them and be prepared.
- Relax and prepare to listen to the instructions
- If you have any physical problem that may keep you from doing your best, be sure to tell the test administrator. If you are sick or in poor health, you really cannot do your best on the exam. You can come back and take the test some other time.

VII. AT THE TEST

The day of the test is here and you have the test booklet in your hand. The temptation to get going is very strong. Caution! There is more to success than knowing the right answers. You must know how to identify your papers and understand variations in the type of short-answer question used in this particular examination. Follow these suggestions for maximum results from your efforts:

1) Cooperate with the monitor

The test administrator has a duty to create a situation in which you can be as much at ease as possible. He will give instructions, tell you when to begin, check to see that you are marking your answer sheet correctly, and so on. He is not there to guard you, although he will see that your competitors do not take unfair advantage. He wants to help you do your best.

2) Listen to all instructions

Don't jump the gun! Wait until you understand all directions. In most civil service tests you get more time than you need to answer the questions. So don't be in a hurry. Read each word of instructions until you clearly understand the meaning. Study the examples, listen to all announcements and follow directions. Ask questions if you do not understand what to do.

3) Identify your papers

Civil service exams are usually identified by number only. You will be assigned a number; you must not put your name on your test papers. Be sure to copy your number correctly. Since more than one exam may be given, copy your exact examination title.

4) Plan your time

Unless you are told that a test is a "speed" or "rate of work" test, speed itself is usually not important. Time enough to answer all the questions will be provided, but this does not mean that you have all day. An overall time limit has been set. Divide the total time (in minutes) by the number of questions to determine the approximate time you have for each question.

5) Do not linger over difficult questions

If you come across a difficult question, mark it with a paper clip (useful to have along) and come back to it when you have been through the booklet. One caution if you do this – be sure to skip a number on your answer sheet as well. Check often to be sure that you have not lost your place and that you are marking in the row numbered the same as the question you are answering.

6) Read the questions

Be sure you know what the question asks! Many capable people are unsuccessful because they failed to read the questions correctly.

7) Answer all questions

Unless you have been instructed that a penalty will be deducted for incorrect answers, it is better to guess than to omit a question.

8) Speed tests

It is often better NOT to guess on speed tests. It has been found that on timed tests people are tempted to spend the last few seconds before time is called in marking answers at random – without even reading them – in the hope of picking up a few extra points. To discourage this practice, the instructions may warn you that your score will be "corrected" for guessing. That is, a penalty will be applied. The incorrect answers will be deducted from the correct ones, or some other penalty formula will be used.

9) Review your answers

If you finish before time is called, go back to the questions you guessed or omitted to give them further thought. Review other answers if you have time.

10) Return your test materials

If you are ready to leave before others have finished or time is called, take ALL your materials to the monitor and leave quietly. Never take any test material with you. The monitor can discover whose papers are not complete, and taking a test booklet may be grounds for disqualification.

VIII. EXAMINATION TECHNIQUES

1) Read the general instructions carefully. These are usually printed on the first page of the exam booklet. As a rule, these instructions refer to the timing of the examination; the fact that you should not start work until the signal and must stop work at a signal, etc. If there are any special instructions, such as a choice of questions to be answered, make sure that you note this instruction carefully.

2) When you are ready to start work on the examination, that is as soon as the signal has been given, read the instructions to each question booklet, underline any key words or phrases, such as least, best, outline, describe and the like. In this way you will tend to answer as requested rather than discover on reviewing your paper that you listed without describing, that you selected the worst choice rather than the best choice, etc.

3) If the examination is of the objective or multiple-choice type – that is, each question will also give a series of possible answers: A, B, C or D, and you are called upon to select the best answer and write the letter next to that answer on your answer paper – it is advisable to start answering each question in turn. There may be anywhere from 50 to 100 such questions in the three or four hours allotted and you can see how much time would be taken if you read through all the questions before beginning to answer any. Furthermore, if you

come across a question or group of questions which you know would be difficult to answer, it would undoubtedly affect your handling of all the other questions.

4) If the examination is of the essay type and contains but a few questions, it is a moot point as to whether you should read all the questions before starting to answer any one. Of course, if you are given a choice – say five out of seven and the like – then it is essential to read all the questions so you can eliminate the two that are most difficult. If, however, you are asked to answer all the questions, there may be danger in trying to answer the easiest one first because you may find that you will spend too much time on it. The best technique is to answer the first question, then proceed to the second, etc.

5) Time your answers. Before the exam begins, write down the time it started, then add the time allowed for the examination and write down the time it must be completed, then divide the time available somewhat as follows:
    - If 3-1/2 hours are allowed, that would be 210 minutes. If you have 80 objective-type questions, that would be an average of 2-1/2 minutes per question. Allow yourself no more than 2 minutes per question, or a total of 160 minutes, which will permit about 50 minutes to review.
    - If for the time allotment of 210 minutes there are 7 essay questions to answer, that would average about 30 minutes a question. Give yourself only 25 minutes per question so that you have about 35 minutes to review.

6) The most important instruction is to read each question and make sure you know what is wanted. The second most important instruction is to time yourself properly so that you answer every question. The third most important instruction is to answer every question. Guess if you have to but include something for each question. Remember that you will receive no credit for a blank and will probably receive some credit if you write something in answer to an essay question. If you guess a letter – say "B" for a multiple-choice question – you may have guessed right. If you leave a blank as an answer to a multiple-choice question, the examiners may respect your feelings but it will not add a point to your score. Some exams may penalize you for wrong answers, so in such cases only, you may not want to guess unless you have some basis for your answer.

7) Suggestions
    a. Objective-type questions
        1. Examine the question booklet for proper sequence of pages and questions
        2. Read all instructions carefully
        3. Skip any question which seems too difficult; return to it after all other questions have been answered
        4. Apportion your time properly; do not spend too much time on any single question or group of questions
        5. Note and underline key words – all, most, fewest, least, best, worst, same, opposite, etc.
        6. Pay particular attention to negatives
        7. Note unusual option, e.g., unduly long, short, complex, different or similar in content to the body of the question
        8. Observe the use of "hedging" words – probably, may, most likely, etc.

9. Make sure that your answer is put next to the same number as the question
10. Do not second-guess unless you have good reason to believe the second answer is definitely more correct
11. Cross out original answer if you decide another answer is more accurate; do not erase until you are ready to hand your paper in
12. Answer all questions; guess unless instructed otherwise
13. Leave time for review

b. Essay questions
   1. Read each question carefully
   2. Determine exactly what is wanted. Underline key words or phrases.
   3. Decide on outline or paragraph answer
   4. Include many different points and elements unless asked to develop any one or two points or elements
   5. Show impartiality by giving pros and cons unless directed to select one side only
   6. Make and write down any assumptions you find necessary to answer the questions
   7. Watch your English, grammar, punctuation and choice of words
   8. Time your answers; don't crowd material

8) Answering the essay question

Most essay questions can be answered by framing the specific response around several key words or ideas. Here are a few such key words or ideas:

M's: manpower, materials, methods, money, management
P's: purpose, program, policy, plan, procedure, practice, problems, pitfalls, personnel, public relations

a. Six basic steps in handling problems:
   1. Preliminary plan and background development
   2. Collect information, data and facts
   3. Analyze and interpret information, data and facts
   4. Analyze and develop solutions as well as make recommendations
   5. Prepare report and sell recommendations
   6. Install recommendations and follow up effectiveness

b. Pitfalls to avoid
1. Taking things for granted – A statement of the situation does not necessarily imply that each of the elements is necessarily true; for example, a complaint may be invalid and biased so that all that can be taken for granted is that a complaint has been registered
2. Considering only one side of a situation – Wherever possible, indicate several alternatives and then point out the reasons you selected the best one
3. Failing to indicate follow up – Whenever your answer indicates action on your part, make certain that you will take proper follow-up action to see how successful your recommendations, procedures or actions turn out to be
4. Taking too long in answering any single question – Remember to time your answers properly

EXAMINATION SECTION

EXAMINATION SECTION
TEST 1

DIRECTIONS: Each question or incomplete statement is followed by several suggested answers or completions. Select the one that BEST answers the question or completes the statement. *PRINT THE LETTER OF THE CORRECT ANSWER IN THE SPACE AT THE RIGHT.*

1. _____ linguistics is a branch of the study of linguistics that deals with evolution of languages, or how languages grow and change. 1.____

    A. Historical B. Socio-
    C. Comparative D. Descriptive

2. The first and oldest branch of the study of anthropology is 2.____

    A. cultural anthropology B. anthropological linguistics
    C. archaeology D. physical anthropology

3. The custom in some cultures which favors the remarriage of a widow to her deceased husband's brother is called 3.____

    A. sodality B. sororate
    C. levirate D. patrilocality

4. Emics are 4.____

    A. the ways in which cultural traits contribute toward maintenance, efficiency, and adaptation of the cultural system
    B. descriptions or judgments concerning behavior, customs, values, etc. that are held by members of a societal group to be culturally appropriate and valid
    C. patterns of behavior associated with specific statuses within a societal group
    D. techniques and results of making generalizations about cultural events, behavior patterns, artifacts, and thought that aim to be cross-culturally valid

5. The earliest known transition from the hunting/gathering way of life into a Neolithic tradition occurred in 5.____

    A. Northern China B. the Middle East
    C. the Indus Valley D. the Nile Valley

6. The distinguishing feature of the state is its 6.____

    A. power to coerce B. stratified society
    C. centralization D. dependence on industry

7. What is the term for the division of a society into two social categories or groups? 7.____

    A. Moiety B. Diglossia
    C. Cleavage D. Dichotomy

8. Which of the following is NOT a trait shared by all living primates? 8.____

    A. A generalized skeleton B. Keen vision
    C. An opposable thumb D. Increased brain size

9. Which of the following fields of study is a branch of physical anthropology?

   A. Prehistoric archaeology
   B. Primatology
   C. Economics
   D. Kinship

10. Presently, some physical anthropologists hypothesize that no known australopithecine was ancestral to the Homo genus. The most significant problem with this hypothesis is that

   A. absolute dating has clearly shown the relative sequence of these fossil hominids
   B. it is based on a hypothetical common ancestor that has yet to be discovered
   C. it ignores the widely accepted theory of natural selection
   D. a link between A. africanus and H. habilis has been firmly established

11. Which of the following tool-making traditions characterize the Lower Paleolithic?
   I. Aurignacian
   II. Achuelian
   III. Mousterian
   IV. Oldowan

   The CORRECT answer is:

   A. I only
   B. II only
   C. I, III
   D. II, IV

12. Which of the following anthropological terms is used to describe a relationship based on marriage?

   A. Matrineal
   B. Nuptial
   C. Consanguineal
   D. Affinal

13. The humans species' way of adapting to the wider environment is termed

   A. culture
   B. biological instincts
   C. mutation
   D. natural selection

14. In an industrial economy, which of the following sectors is devoted to the processing of raw materials into manufactured goods?

   A. Primary
   B. Secondary
   C. Tertiary
   D. Quaternary

15. The term *idiom* is used to name a kind of linguistic

   A. metaphor
   B. denotation
   C. schema
   D. prototype

16. In a very general way, the Neolithic period can be characterized as an age of cultural systems that

   A. featured an enlarged and refined repertory of core and flake tools
   B. produced the world's first cities
   C. were based on domesticated plants and animals
   D. produced tools and works of art from ivory, bone, and antler

17. Which of the following is the hominoid that appears earliest in the fossil record?

   A. Ramapithecus
   B. Proconsul
   C. Gigantopithecus
   D. Aegyptopithecus

18. What is the term for a group based on nonkinship principles? 18.____

    A. Band B. Clan C. Sororate D. Sodality

19. Which of the following is NOT typically a category of economic exchange discussed by anthropologists? 19.____

    A. Redistributive B. Market
    C. Subsistent D. Reciprocal

20. Of the following, which is/are common criticisms of the theoretical perspective of cultural ecology? 20.____
    I. It ignores historical and political factors.
    II. As a model, it does not accommodate cultural changes very well.
    III. It reduces human behavior to simple adaptations to the external environment.
    The CORRECT answer is:

    A. I only B. I, II C. I, III D. II, III

21. Which of the following is NOT an ecological event or trend associated with the Mesolithic period? 21.____
    The

    A. domestication of dogs
    B. spread of birch and pine over western Europe
    C. increased reliance on riverine and maritime sources of food
    D. proliferation of megafauna - mammoth, woolly rhinoceros, giant elk, etc. - across the Eurasian grasslands

22. Which of the following customs is most common among Eurasian economies based on intense agriculture? 22.____

    A. Dowry B. Bride price
    C. Groom price D. Bride service

23. A characteristic shared by organisms as the result of common evolutionary descent is a(n) 23.____

    A. analogy B. genotype
    C. homology D. zygote

24. Which of the following types of political organizations is most centralized? 24.____

    A. Chiefdom B. Tribe C. Lineage D. Band

25. In which part of Europe did the transition to the first state forms of government first occur? 25.____

    A. Western/Iberian B. Northern/Anglo-Saxon
    C. Eastern D. Southern

KEY (CORRECT ANSWERS)

1. A
2. D
3. C
4. B
5. B

6. A
7. A
8. C
9. B
10. B

11. D
12. D
13. A
14. B
15. D

16. C
17. D
18. D
19. C
20. C

21. D
22. A
23. C
24. A
25. D

———

TEST 2

DIRECTIONS: Each question or incomplete statement is followed by several suggested answers or completions. Select the one that BEST answers the question or completes the statement. *PRINT THE LETTER OF THE CORRECT ANSWER IN THE SPACE AT THE RIGHT.*

1. Human beings can talk about absent or nonexistent objects and past or future events as easily as they discuss their immediate situations. This is a design feature of the human language known as

    A. signification
    B. displacement
    C. semanticity
    D. symbology

    1.____

2. Bergmann's rule states that

    A. species in equatorial regions have skin that is more darkly pigmented
    B. culture is the dominant criterion by which people form groups
    C. warm-blooded species tend to develop larger, heavier bodies in the colder limits of their range
    D. language is the dominant factor in a group's culture

    2.____

3. In examining language, questions of connotation and denotation fall within the study of

    A. semantics
    B. syntax
    C. idiomatics
    D. grammar

    3.____

4. The field of archaeology, in its examination of material remains, has typically maintained a(n) _____ focus in its studies.

    A. cultural
    B. linguistic
    C. physical
    D. holistic

    4.____

5. Which of the following are NOT paralinguistic elements?

    A. Vocalizations
    B. Vocal characterizers
    C. Form classes
    D. Voice qualities

    5.____

6. Over time, physical anthropology has also become known by the term

    A. palynology
    B. primatology
    C. sociocultural anthropology
    D. biological anthropology

    6.____

7. In nonindustrial societies, land resources are most often controlled by

    A. the head of a nuclear family
    B. an elected chief
    C. whoever occupies the land at a given time
    D. kinship groups

    7.____

5

8. The major goal of contemporary anthropological archaeology is to
   A. explain the archaeological record in a systematic, interactive context
   B. describe and classify materials
   C. speculate on the events of the past
   D. explain cultural phenomena through broad inquiry

9. In anthropological applications, the institution of marriage is defined primarily in terms of
   A. sexual access   B. social forces
   C. economics   D. religious commitment

10. The disappearance of a group (usually a minority group) through the loss of biological and/or cultural distinctiveness is a process known as
    A. adsorption   B. assimilation
    C. anabolism   D. absorption

11. Some anthropologists believe that the reason for the incest taboo, universally strong in nearly all the world's cultures, is solely biological in nature, a device for precluding the harmful effects of inbreeding.
    Which of the following statements, if true, does the most to weaken this hypothesis?
    A. Most victims of incest who are young girls are too young to bring a healthy, fully developed child to term.
    B. Without genetic diversity, a species cannot adapt biologically to a changed environment when and if it becomes necessary.
    C. Children raised together communally, in environments such as an Israeli kibbutz, almost invariably marry outside their group, though they are not required or even encouraged to do so.
    D. Inbreeding can be used to increase desired characteristics as well as deleterious ones.

12. Which of the following procedures in archaeological fieldwork is typically performed FIRST?
    A. Conducting site surveys
    B. Performing test excavations
    C. Determining why a site should be dug
    D. Selecting a particular site

13. In most societies without theistic religions, dangerous situations, or any situation in which a person's knowledge or practical powers are inadequate, will usually elicit the practice of
    A. prayer   B. divination
    C. magic   D. abandonment

14. When a society acquires new traits on a large scale as a result of direct contact with another culture, _____ has occurred.
    A. enculturation   B. diffusion
    C. acculturation   D. assimilation

15. In Hindu society, the *sacred cow* is forbidden as food. Some anthropologists have theorized that this is not simply because of religious reasons, but because the cow was more sensibly put to use as a draft animal.
    The theory which offers this explanation is

    A. cultural ecology B. cultural evolution
    C. functionalism D. cultural determinism

16. According to Wallace's typology of religions, which type represents the simplest form of religious practice?

    A. Communal B. Olympian
    C. Shamanic D. Monotheistic

17. Carrying capacity is the

    A. maximum amount of cultural infiltration a group can absorb until all boundary maintenance has been lost
    B. number of species into which a taxonomic genus can be subdivided until a new genus must be created
    C. maximum population of a species that a particular eco-system can support under a specific set of conditions
    D. number of class stratifications that a certain society can maintain before a new, separate society has been created

18. The discovery of Australopithecus boisei has been important mostly as an illustration of

    A. the line of demarcation between australopithecines and the Homo genus
    B. the importance of bipedalism
    C. the transition from robust to gracile australopithecines
    D. variation within early hominids

19. The most obvious demographic effect of the Neolithic period was a(n)

    A. decrease in infant mortality
    B. increase in literacy
    C. rapid increase in total population
    D. overall increase in life expectancy

20. The major characteristic that differentiates hominids from other primate species is

    A. the opposable thumb B. a high cranial vault
    C. bipedalism D. the clavicle

21. The assumption that in cultural phenomena, similar causes under similar conditions give rise to similar effects, is known as

    A. determinism B. behaviorism
    C. animism D. structuralism

22. The kinship group with which most Americans are familiar is the

    A. bilateral descent group B. bifurcation
    C. bilateral kindred D. unilineal descent group

23. The process of describing individual cultures or societies—largely through the direct interaction with the people concerned—is called

    A. ethnography
    B. populology
    C. ethnology
    D. fieldwork

24. A religious ritual that takes place during a real or potential crisis for a group is termed a rite of

    A. passage
    B. exigency
    C. intensification
    D. appeasement

25. Among other significations, the transition from the Lower Paleolithic to the Middle Paleolithic is marked on the archaeological record by the emergence of the cores and flakes described as

    A. Solutrean
    B. Levalloisian
    C. Magdalenian
    D. Chatelperronian

KEY (CORRECT ANSWERS)

1.	B	11.	C
2.	C	12.	C
3.	A	13.	C
4.	A	14.	C
5.	C	15.	A
6.	D	16.	C
7.	D	17.	C
8.	D	18.	D
9.	A	19.	C
10.	B	20.	C

21. A
22. C
23. A
24. C
25. B

TEST 3

DIRECTIONS: Each question or incomplete statement is followed by several suggested answers or completions. Select the one that BEST answers the question or completes the statement. *PRINT THE LETTER OF THE CORRECT ANSWER IN THE SPACE AT THE RIGHT.*

1. One theory of speciation holds that evolutionary changes are triggered by species-forming events which may occur within a regularly short span of time. This is the theory of 1.____

    A. independent assortment B. punctuated equilibrium
    C. redistribution D. phyletic gradualism

2. The best explanation of a schema's purpose is to 2.____

    A. make language less ambiguous
    B. place events, experiences, or relationships into a culturally relevant semantic domain
    C. decode meaning relationships such as synonymy, homophony, and antonymy
    D. make events understandable and easier to interpret

3. Which of the following is NOT a science that is fundamental to the study of physical anthropology? 3.____

    A. Biology B. Chemistry
    C. Sociology D. Geology

4. In which of the following types of kinship systems are all relatives of the same sex and generation referred to by the same term? 4.____

    A. Crow B. Hawaiian
    C. Descriptive D. Bilateral

5. The Classic era in the development of Mesoamerican states is exemplified in the civilization at 5.____

    A. Tula B. Tenochtitlan
    C. Cuicuilco D. Teotihuacan

6. Each of the following statements about the descent group known as a lineage is true EXCEPT it is 6.____

    A. a non-corporate group
    B. usually used to describe some form of unilineal descent
    C. exogamous
    D. ancestor-oriented

7. In some cultures, the activities of a man are restricted during the time of his wife's delivery of their child.
   This restriction is known as 7.____

    A. couvade B. stinting
    C. corveé D. consanguination

8. Of the following types of descent groups, which is considered to be the smallest one that cannot be further sub-divided?

   A. Phratry B. Moiety C. Lineage D. Clan

9. What is the term for the specialized field of anthropology that uses information gathered from the other anthropological specialties to solve practical cross-cultural problems?

   A. Socioeconomic anthropology
   B. Population demographics
   C. Applied anthropology
   D. Ethnology

10. Which of the following geologic ages is most likely to be the time when the first hominids emerged?

    A. Late Eocene
    B. Early Pleistocene
    C. Late Oligocene
    D. Early Pliocene

11. The assertion that language has the power to shape the way people see the world is known as the _____ hypothesis.

    A. Turney-High
    B. Boas
    C. Hardy-Weinberg
    D. Sapir-Whorf

12. Which of the following describes a means of tracing descent through all ancestors, male and female?

    A. Cognatic
    B. Ambilineal
    C. Cosmolineal
    D. Bilineal

13. Which of the following elements of human social organization is NOT associated with foraging?

    A. Camp as the center of daily activity
    B. Sexual division of labor
    C. Redistributive exchange
    D. Sharing of food between adults

14. In the systems approach, the _____ component of prehistoric culture is the major means by which archaeologists come to understand the social organization and ideology of ancient people.

    A. biological
    B. contextual
    C. ecological
    D. technical

15. In a large majority of the world's societies, the preferred form of marriage is

    A. group marriage
    B. monogamy
    C. levirate
    D. polygyny

16. Of the following primate subdivisions, which are NOT hominoids?

    A. Hominids
    B. Cercopithecoids
    C. Hylobatids
    D. Pongids

17. About the concept of organic solidarity, each of the following is true EXCEPT it

    A. is often based on similarities such as language and mode of livelihood
    B. is made up of many greatly specialized groups
    C. depends on a highly developed division of labor
    D. represents a strong interdependence

18. What is the term for the ability to communicate about items or events with which the communicators are not in direct contact?

    A. Conjuring
    B. Displacement
    C. Divination
    D. Abstraction

19. In pantheistic religions of both the present and the past, it is often the case that a supreme deity is acknowledged, and yet is all but totally ignored by the people. The reason for this is usually the belief that

    A. such a remote god is unlikely to be interested or directly involved in human affairs
    B. this god had creative powers, but no power to influence human life once it was begun
    C. to attract the attention of the supreme deity will bring about unwelcome change
    D. there is no afterlife, or form of divine reward or punishment, following the earthly life

20. The theoretical perspective of cultural ecology focuses on areas distinguished by particular climates and certain types of plants and animals. These areas are referred to as ecozones or

    A. niches   B. meridians   C. biomes   D. foci

21. Which of the following is NOT a problem commonly associated with nuclear family organizations?

    A. Less help available from the state
    B. Encouraged co-dependence
    C. Anxieties over caring for the elderly
    D. Isolation from kin

22. Thor Heyerdahl's 1950 *Kon-Tiki* expedition, an attempt to support his theory that the Polynesian Islands were populated from the Americas, is an example of

    A. ethnoarchaeology
    B. experimental archaeology
    C. cultural ecology
    D. applied anthropology

23. Rituals can usually be described in each of the following ways EXCEPT

    A. inventive
    B. occurring at set times
    C. stereotyped
    D. stylized

24. Leibig's law points out that in biological evolution,

    A. changes in a given gene pool occur suddenly and cataclysmically, rather than gradually
    B. some genetic traits are dominant over others
    C. the processes of adaptation and selection respond to the given minimal potentialities of the environment
    D. the genotype of an offspring is determined by the alleles of its parents

25. The study of language in the context of its use is known as

    A. semantics
    B. pragmatics
    C. syntax
    D. eponymy

KEY (CORRECT ANSWERS)

1.	B	11.	D
2.	D	12.	A
3.	C	13.	C
4.	B	14.	D
5.	D	15.	D
6.	A	16.	B
7.	A	17.	A
8.	C	18.	B
9.	C	19.	A
10.	D	20.	C

21. B
22. B
23. A
24. C
25. B

TEST 4

DIRECTIONS: Each question or incomplete statement is followed by several suggested answers or completions. Select the one that BEST answers the question or completes the statement. *PRINT THE LETTER OF THE CORRECT ANSWER IN THE SPACE AT THE RIGHT.*

1. The device known as a Punnett square is used to

    A. map out the grid of an archaeological site
    B. plot the relationship between superordinate and sub-ordinate groups in a society
    C. determine the proportion in which genotypes will occur among groups of fathers and mothers
    D. determine kinship ties among a given group

   1.____

2. In virtually all cultures, rites of passage involve a(n)

    A. appeal to ancestral spirits
    B. ritual denial of bodily nourishment
    C. alteration – either real or symbolic – of the individual's physical form
    D. ritual removal of the individual from society

   2.____

3. In the late nineteenth century, Indian tribes throughout the United States conducted ceremonial *Ghost Dances* that were designed to induce the return of Christ as an Indian to America. Once on Earth, it was believed that the new Christ would return the buffalo and running water to the land, and would bury white people beneath the new green grass. The ghost dances were an example of

    A. cultural cross-pollination
    B. a revitalization movement
    C. parallel cultural evolution
    D. animism

   3.____

4. In anthropological terms, the basic residential unit in which a variety of functions - economic production, production, consumption, inheritance, child rearing, and shelter - are organized and carried out is always described by the term

    A. household   B. ménage
    C. family   D. domicile

   4.____

5. The first true primates, the prosimians, first appear in the fossil record during the

    A. Pleistocene   B. Late Cretaceous
    C. Paleocene   D. Eocene

   5.____

6. The earliest recognized tool-making tradition is the

    A. Aurignacian   B. Oldowan
    C. Acheulean   D. Mousterian

   6.____

7. Which of the following is NOT generally true of the Indian caste system?

   A. Particular castes are associated with specific food habits and styles of dress.
   B. Membership is determined by descent.
   C. Particular castes are associated with economic status rather than specific occupations.
   D. Castes are strictly endogamous.

8. The archaeological record indicates that many prehistoric hunter-gatherers seemed to delay the large-scale domestication of animals for food and other functions. The reason for this is most likely that

   A. there were very few animals suitable for domestication in the areas where these people lived
   B. food sources were scarce enough that sharing them with domesticated animals would have created shortages
   C. cultural taboos prevented the close association of people and animals
   D. they did not yet have the knowledge required to raise and breed animals

9. Which of the following can be said to be the ideological opposite of ethnocentrism?

   A. Cultural determinism
   B. Bigotry
   C. Etiology
   D. Cultural relativity

10. Each of the following is considered to be a field of applied anthropology EXCEPT

    A. developmental anthropology
    B. urban anthropology
    C. material life and technology
    D. medical anthropology

11. _____ -cousin marriage is favored in hierarchical societies in which property of interest to men is inherited by daughters as well as sons.

    A. Matrilateral cross
    B. Matrilateral parallel
    C. Patrilateral cross
    D. Patrilateral parallel

12. The practice of animism is

    A. the attribution of humanlike consciousness and powers to inanimate objects, natural phenomena, plants, and animals
    B. the arrival at an expectation or judgment of future events through the interpretation of omens considered to be evidence
    C. the practice of certain rituals that are presumed to coerce desired practical effects in the material world
    D. a belief in personalized yet disembodied beings such as ghosts, souls, spirits, and gods

13. A *liminal* individual undergoing a rite of passage is typically

    A. cut off from normal social contacts
    B. coerced into difficult labor
    C. physically adorned
    D. bestowed new responsibilities

14. The major form of relative dating used with fossilized remains is   14._____

    A. palynology   B. potassium-argon dating
    C. faunal correlation   D. stratigraphic dating

15. Which of the following words could not be used to describe culture?   15._____

    A. Adaptive   B. Shared   C. Innate   D. Symbolic

16. Societies with a highly decentralized and relatively egalitarian form of political organiza-   16._____
    tion are often described as

    A. democratic   B. communal
    C. acephalous   D. animated

17. Which of the following statements is FALSE?   17._____

    A. A tear is a signal of crying.
    B. A traffic light is a symbol for one of a set of commands.
    C. The word *car* is a symbol for an object.
    D. A wave is a signal of greeting.

18. In the late nineteenth century, it was the predominant view that all cultures evolved in the   18._____
    same order through a series of stages. This form of cultural evolution was referred to as

    A. unilinear   B. convergent
    C. multilinear   D. specific

19. The *berdache* of native North American societies – usually a male transvestite who   19._____
    assumed a sanctioned female role among his people – is an example of a

    A. nonproductive role   B. supernumerary sex
    C. phenotypic difference   D. supernumerary gender

20. The basic premise of the *middle range* theory of ethnographic analogy is that   20._____

    A. the archaeological record is a static, unchanging representation of the dynamic
       processes of culture and behavior
    B. studying contemporary foraging cultures is the best way to understand the hunter-
       gatherers of the past
    C. if similar or identical objects are found at different levels within a single archaeolog-
       ical site, they should be dated as if they appeared exactly halfway between the two
    D. archaeologists can better understand the technical abilities and reasoning pro-
       cesses of ancient people by reproducing their actions

21. Which of the following is NOT a design element of human language?   21._____

    A. Semanticity
    B. Singularity of patterning
    C. Prevarication
    D. Arbitrariness

22. Which of the following is a term for the basic genetically determined propensities for   22._____
    behavior characteristics of a species?

    A. Biogram   B. Bent
    C. Divination   D. Allele

23. In linguistics, the purpose of frame substitution is to

    A. identify the syntactic units of language
    B. divide vocal sounds into the smallest possible units of meaning
    C. determine whether a morpheme is free or bound
    D. illustrate semantic relationships

24. Which of the following is NOT considered to be one of the fundamental aspects of culture?

    A. Material
    B. Cognitive
    C. Comparative
    D. Behavioral

25. Which of the following is an example of a redistributive economic exchange in the modern United States?

    A. A garage sale
    B. *Conspicuous consumption*
    C. The purchase of a new automobile
    D. Taxes

KEY (CORRECT ANSWERS)

1. C		11. D	
2. D		12. D	
3. B		13. A	
4. A		14. D	
5. D		15. C	
6. B		16. C	
7. C		17. D	
8. B		18. A	
9. D		19. D	
10. C		20. A	

21. B
22. A
23. A
24. C
25. D

TEST 5

DIRECTIONS: Each question or incomplete statement is followed by several suggested answers or completions. Select the one that BEST answers the question or completes the statement. *PRINT THE LETTER OF THE CORRECT ANSWER IN THE SPACE AT THE RIGHT.*

1. The practice of applied anthropology most often concerns

   A. physical anthropologists
   B. linguists
   C. cultural anthropologists
   D. archaeologists

   1.____

2. Mary Leakey's discovery of fossilized hominid footprints at the Laetoli site in Tanzania was significant because it confirmed that

   A. early hominids used a combination of bipedalism and knuckle-walking
   B. younger australopithecines were capable of independent locomotion
   C. australopithecines generally ate their food where they found it
   D. fully bipedal creatures existed between 3 and 4 million years ago

   2.____

3. The principle that all cultural systems are inherently equal in value, and that the traits and characteristics of each need to be assessed and explained within the context of the system in which they occur, is the principle of cultural

   A. determinism   B. relativism
   C. materialism   D. evolution

   3.____

4. Which of the following was a Miocene ape whose fossils have appeared in China, Vietnam, Pakistan, and Northern India?

   A. Gigantopithecus   B. B, Ramapithecus
   C. Proconsul   D. Dryopithecus

   4.____

5. In the archaeological record, the _____ period is characterized by a marked increase in blade tools and by a great florescence of ivory, bone, and antler implements.

   A. Lower Paleolithic   B. Upper Paleolithic
   C. Mesolithic   D. Neolithic

   5.____

6. A member of a society in which animal husbandry is regarded as the ideal way of life, and in which movement of all or part of the society is considered a normal and natural way of life, is defined as a

   A. rancher   B. nomad
   C. forager   D. pastoralist

   6.____

7. The cladistic approach to taxonomy

   A. eliminates the need to distinguish among closely related species
   B. focuses on the differences between species
   C. relies more on phenotypes than genotypes
   D. graphically represents the variation of certain traits over geographical space

   7.____

8. Which of the following is a trait that differentiates the teeth of most australopithecines from those of modern humans?

   A. Sharper incisors
   B. Extremely large molars
   C. Thicker enamel
   D. Nonexistent canine teeth

9. The archaeological record indicates that the last independent state within the Valley of Mexico belonged to the

   A. Toltecs   B. Mayans   C. Aztecs   D. Olmecs

10. The test of the adequacy of etic descriptions of a culture is whether they

    A. fully express the uniqueness of society's infrastructure
    B. generatescientific theories about the causes of socio-cultural differences and similarities
    C. eliminate the need for further ethnographic studies
    D. correspond with a view of the world that natives accept as real and meaningful

11. The rule that forbids an individual from taking a spouse from within a proscribed group with which they are both affiliated is called

    A. endogamy   B. polygamy   C. exogamy   D. bigamy

12. In the evolution of religious practice, which of the following types of religious practice has been found most commonly among foragers?

    A. Communal
    B. Olympian
    C. Shamanic
    D. Monotheistic

13. The final stage in the domestication of a plant occurs when

    A. ripe grains must be pulled or beaten off in order to be available for consumption
    B. the domesticate is removed from its natural habitat to an area that is markedly different
    C. the plant is incapable of reproducing itself without human assistance
    D. the plant is genetically altered into a form more easily sown and harvested

14. Internalized forms of social control are typically rooted in

    A. fear of punishment
    B. adopted mores
    C. the possibility of reward
    D. inherent beliefs

15. Among the Upper Paleolithic traditions in Western Europe, which of the following is generally considered to be the oldest?

    A. Chatelperronian
    B. Magdalenian
    C. Gravettian
    D. Solutrean

16. Which of the following paleoanthropologists discovered the first fossilized record of Homo habilis in Olduvai Gorge?

    A. Mary Leakey
    B. Robert Broom
    C. Raymond Dart
    D. Richard Leakey

17. A morpheme is

    A. a single vocal sound which a listener recognizes as having a certain linguistic function
    B. the smallest sequence of sounds to which a definite meaning can be attached
    C. individual units of sound that contrast with one another
    D. the characteristics of an individual organism that are the external, apparent manifestation of its hereditary genetic composition

18. Each of the following is a likely reason for the gradual formalization of law enforcement as societies progressed from hunter-gatherers to organized states EXCEPT the

    A. central importance of kinship groups and domestic groups in the social organization of early societies
    B. gradual erosion of moral codes and imperatives as societies became more complex
    C. increasing size of the society
    D. absence of marked inequalities in access to technology and resources

19. The field of descriptive linguistics is concerned primarily with

    A. the relationship between language and social factors such as class, ethnicity, age, and gender
    B. how languages are constructed and how the various parts are interrelated to form coherent systems of communication
    C. the ways in which languages affect how people think, and how beliefs and values influence linguistic patterns
    D. the growth and change of languages over time

20. In societies where the belief in ancestral spirits exists, these spirits are

    A. almost universally benevolent
    B. believed to behave predictably, in ways that mirror the events of family life
    C. frequently seen as retaining an active interest and even membership in society
    D. believed to be solely judicious, without appetite or emotion

21. What is the term for artifacts at an archaeological site that are nonportable remnants of human activity, and that cannot be removed intact from a site?

    A. Ecofacts
    B. Durable remains
    C. Features
    D. Fixtures

22. Which of the following theoretical perspectives of anthropology explores the relationships among a society's different institutions and how these institutions serve society or the individual?

    A. Cultural ecology
    B. Functionalism
    C. Cultural determinism
    D. Structuralism

23. Among the Old World monkeys, the two subfamilies—cercopithecines and colbbines—differ most starkly in

   A. their diet
   B. size
   C. their geographic distribution
   D. their method of locomotion

24. The determination of descent through a combination of male and female ancestors, establishing a descent relationship with a particular ancestor, is a method of reckoning known as

   A. patrimatrilineal descent
   B. bilateral descent
   C. biographing
   D. ambilineal descent

25. Of the following, the clearest example of a sodality is a

   A. nuclear family
   B. native tribe
   C. lineage
   D. priestly society

KEY (CORRECT ANSWERS)

1. C
2. D
3. B
4. A
5. B

6. D
7. A
8. B
9. C
10. B

11. C
12. C
13. B
14. D
15. A

16. D
17. B
18. B
19. B
20. C

21. C
22. B
23. A
24. D
25. D

EXAMINATION SECTION
TEST 1

DIRECTIONS: Each question or incomplete statement is followed by several suggested answers or completions. Select the one that BEST answers the question or completes the statement. *PRINT THE LETTER OF THE CORRECT ANSWER IN THE SPACE AT THE RIGHT.*

1. The human achievements of the Mesolithic period are believed to include each of the following EXCEPT

    A. great cave paintings of big-game animals and ceremonial rites
    B. the development of a wide range of fishing gear
    C. an array of specialized tips fashioned for projectile weapons
    D. geometric designs and symbols incised on tools, weapons, and painted pebbles

1.____

2. In terms of regulating the way land resources are used, pastoralists require a method of determining

    A. who can hunt game and gather plants, and where these activities will take place
    B. how farmland is to be acquired, worked, and passed on
    C. rights to water and grazing land
    D. private ownership of land and rights

2.____

3. Which of the following is true of an ascribed group?

    A. Criteria for membership are largely economic.
    B. Membership is usually voluntary.
    C. Membership is acquired at birth.
    D. Most religious groups are ascribed groups.

3.____

4. The act of sticking pins into a *voodoo doll* is an example of

    A. divination   B. sympathetic magic
    C. channeling   D. contagious magic

4.____

5. Each of the following is considered to be a synonym for the term *cultural anthropology* EXCEPT

    A. sociocultural anthropology
    B. ethnology
    C. ethnography
    D. social anthropology

5.____

6. Steno's law of superposition states that

    A. in the evolution of hominids, a smaller cranial vault will belong to those lowest on the ancestral tree
    B. in any succession of rock layers, the lowest rocks are the oldest
    C. any anthropoid creature in the fossil record that can be proven to have used tools is automatically classified in the Homo genus
    D. in any developed state, there is at least one group that exerts political and economic dominance

6.____

7. In order to determine whether a fossilized primate was bipedal, paleoanthropologists examine the orientation of the opening in the back of the skull through which the spinal cord passes. The term for this opening is

   A. sagittal crest
   B. foramen magnum
   C. cranial vault
   D. fontanel

8. What is the term for a social relationship based on presumed biological links?

   A. Kinship
   B. Consanguinity
   C. Community
   D. Affinity

9. The basic premise of cultural determinism is that

   A. mind and body, individuals and society, and individuals and the environment interpenetrate and help to define one another
   B. the important material forces that shape our world lie outside our bodies in the surrounding world
   C. the ideas, meanings, and beliefs that we learn as members of society become the definitive agents of the human condition
   D. the material activities of our physical bodies in the material world are the essence of human nature

10. The term *Fertile Crescent* is used to describe a geographical region within

    A. Central and Eastern Europe
    B. Mesoamerica
    C. the Asian alluvial fan of the Himalayas
    D. Africa and the Middle East

11. As a theory, linguistic determinism has a number of problems. Which of the following is NOT one of them?

    A. It is almost universally possible to translate from one language to another.
    B. There are languages in which only one third-person pronoun in the language is used for males and females, despite patriarchal social patterns in the culture speaking them.
    C. Culture intimately associated with natural phenomena, such as the Inuit, have developed numerous ways of describing objects or patterns that are nearly indistinguishable to outsiders.
    D. People who grow up bilingual do not have two contradictory views of reality.

12. What is the term for the impersonal pervasive power which, in certain cultures, is expected in certain objects and roles?

    A. Mana   B. Taxon   C. Neem   D. Anima

13. Reciprocity can be said to be characteristic of societies that are relatively

    A. nomadic
    B. egalitarian
    C. religious
    D. industrialized

14. Which of the following trends or events most clearly caused the creation of states in Northern Europe?
The

   A. conflict of barbarian chiefdoms with the Roman Empire
   B. use of megalithic religious monuments
   C. storage of grains and livestock
   D. trade in copper and bronze objects

15. Which of the following can be said to be the basis of social-class structure in human societies?

   A. Population management
   B. Resource distribution
   C. Technological achievement
   D. Role differentiation

16. The most fundamental cause of the cultural changes associated with the Neolithic period appears to have been

   A. a proliferation of varied fauna across the Levant
   B. climatic changes that produced long, hot, arid summers
   C. an increased reliance on perennial plants
   D. clashes over scarce resources

17. Which of the following is NOT a characteristic of most primate social groups?

   A. Sexual monogamy   B. Dominance hierarchy
   C. Violence   D. Social grooming

18. In general, when a people have changed from foraging to a food-producing way of life, their religion has undergone a transformation from

   A. zoomorphic to anthropomorphic gods
   B. totemism to theism
   C. shamanism to pantheism
   D. polytheism to monotheism

19. Symbols that bear a direct resemblance to the items they symbolize are described as

   A. uncoded   B. iconographic
   C. metaphorical   D. iconoclastic

20. Among newly married couples, ambilocal residences are particularly well-suited to situations in which

   A. economic cooperation of more people than are available in the nuclear family is needed, but where resources are limited in some way
   B. ecological circumstances make the role of the woman prominent in subsistence
   C. descent through women is deemed crucial for the transmission of important rights and property
   D. the independence of the nuclear family is emphasized

21. The vast majority of features used to differentiate the hominoids from other anthropoids in the fossil record, and to distinguish among the various types of hominoids, relate primarily to
    A. overall skeletal structure
    B. the brow ridge
    C. dentition
    D. the cranial vault

21.____

22. Which of the following is NOT a characteristic of the food-foraging life?
    A. Populations stabilize in numbers well below carrying capacity of the land
    B. Hierarchical social order within groups
    C. Small (25-50 on average) local groups
    D. Constantly shifting social density

22.____

23. Which of the following is a microevolutionary pattern in which different species evolve similar traits as a result of functional adaptations to similar environmental conditions?
    A. Convergence   B. Radiation
    C. Cladism   D. Brachiation

23.____

24. Which of the following types of kinship systems emphasizes the nuclear family by specifically identifying mother, father, brother, and sister, while merging together all other relatives?
    A. Eskimo   B. Hawaiian   C. Crow   D. Iroquois

24.____

25. Which of the following procedures in archaeological fieldwork is typically performed LAST?
    A. Site sampling   B. Digging a control pit
    C. Mapping the site   D. Conducting site surveys

25.____

KEY (CORRECT ANSWERS)

1.	A	11.	C
2.	C	12.	A
3.	C	13.	B
4.	B	14.	A
5.	C	15.	D
6.	B	16.	B
7.	B	17.	A
8.	B	18.	A
9.	C	19.	B
10.	D	20.	A

21. C
22. B
23. A
24. A
25. A

TEST 2

DIRECTIONS: Each question or incomplete statement is followed by several suggested answers or completions. Select the one that BEST answers the question or completes the statement. *PRINT THE LETTER OF THE CORRECT ANSWER IN THE SPACE AT THE RIGHT.*

1. Which of the following statements about modern monotheistic religions is generally FALSE?

    A. The role of priests has declined.
    B. Notions of the afterlife have been de-emphasized.
    C. Salvation is directly available to individuals.
    D. They are *world-rejecting* religions.

2. A language with no native speakers, that develops within a single generation between members of communities that possess distinct native languages, is known as a(n)

    A. argot   B. creole   C. pidgin   D. dialect

3. Among Australian natives, it is often the practice for hunters to divide meat among the families of the hunters and other relatives, with each person in the camp receiving a share. This is an example of

    A. a leveling mechanism   B. generalized reciprocity
    C. redistribution   D. balanced reciprocity

4. In kin terminology, first cousins would be described as

    A. bilateral   B. affinal
    C. collateral   D. parallel

5. The reasons for the relative rarity of polyandry among people include each of the following EXCEPT

    A. male infant mortality runs at a higher rate
    B. its poor way to subdivide scant resources through inheritance
    C. male life expectancy is shorter
    D. it limits a man's descendants more than any other marriage pattern

6. Each of the following is a type of regulatory subsystem that is found within all states EXCEPT

    A. population control   B. lineal
    C. fiscal   D. judiciary

7. Of the following, what type of people are more likely to form egalitarian societies?

    A. Nomadic warriors   B. Sedentary farmers
    C. Technologically advanced   D. Food foragers

8. The factor which is of primary interest to those who study cultural ecology is

    A. reproduction   B. evolution
    C. assimilation   D. adaptation

9. What is the term for the cultural construction of behaviors and beliefs considered appropriate for each sex?

   A. Guild
   B. Gender
   C. Neuter
   D. Sex roles

10. According to Tylor and most other anthropologists who study religion, the evolution of religion began with

    A. monotheism
    B. agnosticism
    C. polytheism
    D. animism

11. Descriptions or judgments concerning behavior, customs, beliefs, values, and so on, held by members of a societal group as culturally appropriate and valid, are known as

    A. labels
    B. mores
    C. emics
    D. norms

12. Which of the following is an explanation of misfortune based on the belief that certain individuals possess an innate, psychic power capable of causing harm?

    A. Magic
    B. Witchcraft
    C. Divination
    D. Voodoo

13. In anthropological terms, a band is best described as

    A. associations not based on age, kinship, marriage, or territory that result from an act of joining
    B. a noncorporate descent group with each member claiming descent from a common ancestor
    C. a ranked society in which every member has a position in the hierarchy
    D. a loosely organized group of hunter-gatherer families, occupying a specifiable territory and tending toward self-sufficiency

14. What is the term for externalized social controls that are designed to encourage conformity to social norms?

    A. Laws
    B. Statutes
    C. Propaganda
    D. Sanctions

15. The types of archaeological context regarding a site's durable remains include each of the following EXCEPT

    A. environmental
    B. temporal
    C. cultural
    D. spatial

16. *Joint family* is a name for a family pattern made up of

    A. brothers and their wives or sisters and their husbands (along with their children)
    B. two generations living together - parents and unmarried children
    C. cross- or parallel cousins and their spouses (along with their children)
    D. three generations living together - parents, married children, and grandchildren

17. The type of basic personality perceived to be characteristic of a cultural system is described as its _____ personality.

    A. stereotypical
    B. modal
    C. morphological
    D. normal

18. The most important requirement for the control of disputes in band societies has proven to be the

   A. determination of the truth at the heart of the matter
   B. surreptitious determination of the band's majority opinion on the matter before it is heard before them
   C. temporary insulation of the disputants from the collective response of their respective kin groups
   D. determination of whether the accused transgressor's behavior has violated the moral code of the band

18.___

19. In the archaeological record, the earliest recognizable city is found at

   A. Babylon   B. Uruk
   C. Catal Huyuk   D. Jericho

19.___

20. Which of the following fossil hominids is currently considered to be a common ancestor to all subsequent hominids?

   A. Ramapithecus   B. Australopithecus africanus
   C. Homo erectus   D. Australopithecus afarensis

20.___

21. Generally speaking, which of the following conditions or circumstances are believed to have been shared by each of the world's first independently evolved states?
   I. They were all in arid areas where irrigation had been significant.
   II. They all arose within a period of about 1,000 years.
   III. They began with communities based on food production.
   IV. They each used religion to bolster managerial authority.

   The CORRECT answer is:

   A. II only   B. I, III   C. I, III, IV   D. II, IV

21.___

22. Which of the following is widely applied to stratified, endogamous descent groups?

   A. Band   B. Brood   C. Caste   D. Line

22.___

23. Which of the following fossil hominids proved to be examples of Homo erectus?
   I. The Taung child
   II. *Piltdown* Man
   III. *Java Man*
   IV. *Peking Man*
   The CORRECT answer is:

   A. I only   B. I, III   C. III, IV   D. II, III, IV

23.___

24. Which of the following is NOT a relative dating technique used on fossilized remains?

   A. The FUN trio   B. Dendrochronology
   C. Stratigraphic dating   D. Palynology

24.___

25. Which of the following statements about nuclear families is typically FALSE?
They

    A. receive minimal help from outside in the event of emergencies or catastrophes
    B. are particular to developed post-industrial societies
    C. involve a strong dependence of family members on one another
    D. are well adapted to a life that requires a high degree of mobility

KEY (CORRECT ANSWERS)

1.	B	11.	C
2.	C	12.	B
3.	B	13.	D
4.	C	14.	D
5.	B	15.	C
6.	B	16.	A
7.	D	17.	B
8.	D	18.	C
9.	B	19.	B
10.	D	20.	D

21. C
22. C
23. C
24. B
25. B

TEST 3

DIRECTIONS: Each question or incomplete statement is followed by several suggested answers or completions. Select the one that BEST answers the question or completes the statement. *PRINT THE LETTER OF THE CORRECT ANSWER IN THE SPACE AT THE RIGHT.*

1. The best description of how the Neolithic tradition spread through Europe was beginning in

    A. southern Europe, spreading north to Holland, west to England, and then into southeast and central Europe
    B. England, spreading to central Europe, then outward in all directions
    C. Iberia, straight west to the middle Danube, then north and south, and finally into England and Eurasia
    D. the Bosporus, spreading to Greece, then to central France and the middle Danube, and then to England and Scandinavia

2. Given the apparent absence of material motivations for warfare among prestate societies, the best explanation for such conflict is probably that

    A. it represents an unconscious awareness of the need to control the rate of a small population's growth
    B. primitive people enjoy war as a kind of sport
    C. small autonomous groups are often forced to compete for scarce resources
    D. humans possess an innate tendency to be aggressive

3. All of the artifacts contained within a single component of an archaeological site are known as a(n)

    A. unit   B. montage
    C. aerie   D. assemblage

4. Among the populations of the developed world, the most common form of marriage is monogamy, a trend related primarily to _____ reasons.

    A. religious   B. economic
    C. moral   D. legal

5. In the fossil record, the first mammals that may be related to primates appear during the

    A. Pliocene   B. Eocene   C. Miocene   D. Paleocene

6. In stratified societies, one's social class is typically manifest in each of the following ways EXCEPT

    A. symbolic indicators   B. verbal evaluation
    C. degree of mobility   D. patterns of association

7. Which of the following is an absolute-dating technique that is based on growth rings added annually by trees?

    A. Dendrochronology   B. Glottochronology
    C. Arbochronology   D. Stratigraphy

8. Today, extended families are most likely to be found

   A. among hunter-gatherer societies
   B. in rural agrarian areas
   C. among Asian cultures
   D. in the poorer sections of dense urban areas

9. The most significant difference between domestic cereal grains (such as wheat or barley) and wild ones is that

   A. domesticated grains are more easily digestible by humans
   B. wild grains generally contain smaller-yield seed heads
   C. domesticated grains have a longer growing season
   D. wild grains break from the stalk upon ripening and fall to the ground

10. Allied groups of bands or villages are typically led by leaders known as

    A. lords   B. headmen   C. chiefs   D. kings

11. The earliest well-described hominid is

    A. Australopithecus africanus
    B. Homo erectus
    C. Australopithecus afarensis
    D. Homo habilis

12. One of the theories on the origin of bipedalism focus on the importance this type of locomotion had in freeing the hands to perform other tasks such as transporting food, carrying infants, or using tools. Which of the following, if true, would do the most to weaken this hypothesis?

    A. The earliest bipedal hominids evolved in a primarily forested habitat, with trees from which food could easily be spotted.
    B. The offspring of early hominid ancestors were unable to cling firmly to the mother.
    C. The earliest stone tools date only to 2.4 million years ago, while bipedalism is at least 4 million years old.
    D. Early hominids lived in loosely knit groups, in which each obtained food for himself or herself.

13. The process by which children acquire behavioral patterns and other aspects of their culture through observation, instruction, and reinforcement is known as

    A. assimilation   B. enculturation
    C. acculturation   D. synthesis

14. _____ is a religion that uses nature as a model for building society.

    A. Shamanism   B. Pantheism
    C. Animism   D. Totemism

15. Investigations of the patterns of material life found in different human groups is typically the work of _____ anthropologists.

    A. cultural   B. physical   C. applied   D. biological

16. When the membership of a lineage becomes too large to be manageable, a process known as fission takes place, whereby the lineage is divided into

    A. totems B. clans C. bands D. phratries

17. In ordering archaeological sites, a(n) _____ refers to a pattern characterized by cultural traits dating from the same time and distributed over a broad geographic area.

    A. tradition
    B. tier
    C. horizon
    D. assemblage

18. Which of the following types of religions is most typical of people who see themselves as superior to nature, rather than a mere part of it?

    A. Pantheism
    B. Animism
    C. Totemism
    D. Monotheism

19. What is the term for the total gene complement received by an individual organism from its parents?

    A. Genotype
    B. Allele
    C. Phenotype
    D. Genome

20. To accept the argument that the Nazis in Germany behaved as they did because their culture led them inevitably to it is to accept the position of

    A. cultural determinism
    B. cultural relativity
    C. holism
    D. historical materialism

21. Which of the following steps in analyzing archaeological data is typically performed LAST?

    A. Labeling and recording objects in a field catalogue
    B. Classifying materials into types
    C. Recording where objects were found
    D. Packing and sending materials to laboratories

22. In the evolution of religious practice, which of the following types of religious practice was generally the first to add full-time religious specialists to society?

    A. Communal
    B. Olympian
    C. Shamanic
    D. Monotheistic

23. The Aurignacian was a tool-making tradition

    A. characterized by symmetrical hand axes
    B. which consisted mostly of flake tools
    C. in which raw materials such as bone, antler, and stone were used
    D. consisting of primitive stone tools of limited variety

24. What is the term for a mode of economic exchange in which the giving and receiving are specific for the value of the goods and for the time of their delivery?

    A. Balanced reciprocity
    B. Market exchange
    C. Generalized reciprocity
    D. Speculation

25. In linguistics, the study of how words are put together is known as 25._____

    A. etymology   B. syntax
    C. morphology D. grammar

KEY (CORRECT ANSWERS)

1. A   11. C
2. C   12. C
3. D   13. B
4. B   14. D
5. D   15. A

6. C   16. B
7. A   17. C
8. B   18. D
9. D   19. A
10. C   20. A

21. B
22. B
23. C
24. A
25. C

TEST 4

DIRECTIONS: Each question or incomplete statement is followed by several suggested answers or completions. Select the one that BEST answers the question or completes the statement. *PRINT THE LETTER OF THE CORRECT ANSWER IN THE SPACE AT THE RIGHT.*

1. What is the term for the process by which organisms or cultural elements undergo changes in form or function, in response to threats to their existence and replication?
   A. Adaptation
   B. Assimilation
   C. Acculturation
   D. Evolution

2. Among humans, dependence training is typically associated with the _____ family organization.
   A. extended
   B. nuclear
   C. joint
   D. female-headed

3. Societies in which the tertiary sector of the economy predominates are described as
   A. recessive
   B. post-industrial
   C. developing
   D. primitive

4. Which of the following residential patterns is most common among married couples in North America?
   A. Patrilocal
   B. Ambilocal
   C. Matrilocal
   D. Neolocal

5. Among the Upper Paleolithic traditions in Europe, which of the following, associated with southern Russia and Czechoslovakia, produced the artifacts known as *venus statues*?
   A. Magdalenian
   B. Chatelperronian
   C. Gravettian
   D. Solutrean

6. The institution linking individuals from upper and lower levels in a stratified society is termed
   A. coterie
   B. patronage
   C. ascribed status
   D. clientage

7. Which of the following are characteristics that generally differentiate Old World monkeys from New World monkeys?
   I. Most New World monkeys have prehensile tails.
   II. New World monkeys have broad, flaring noses.
   III. A greater proportion of Old World monkeys are terrestrial.
   The CORRECT answer is:
   A. I only
   B. I, II
   C. II, III
   D. I, II, III

8. The belief that one's future can be read in the pattern of tea leaves at the bottom of the cup is an example of belief in
   A. divination
   B. contagious magic
   C. divine intervention
   D. clairvoyance

9. Plants, animals, phenomena, or objects symbolically associated with particular descent groups as identifying insignia are known as

   A. anima   B. totems   C. mana   D. regalia

10. Generally (but not always) the horticultural way of life and the agricultural way of life are differentiated by the

   A. size of the community
   B. use of irrigation and the plow
   C. level of income generated by crops
   D. practice of domestication

11. The field of forensic anthropology is an application of

   A. linguistic anthropology
   B. primatology
   C. cultural anthropology
   D. physical anthropology

12. Which of the following statements about classes is FALSE?

   A. They often correlate to race and ethnicity.
   B. Boundaries are fluid enough for people to change classes within their lifetimes.
   C. They apply to most large-scale societies of the modern world.
   D. They are not endogamous.

13. A common criticism of the theoretical perspective of functionalism in anthropological study is that it

   A. discounts the influence of religion
   B. does not address the influence of specific institutions on societies
   C. tends to view humans as apolitical beings
   D. fails to explain the differences and similarities between societies

14. Probably the simplest way to define *syntax* is to say it is the study of

   A. grammar
   B. sentence structure
   C. meaning
   D. language

15. The most basic goal of anthropological archaeology is to

   A. reconstruct ancient ways of life
   B. provide evidence for lines of kinship
   C. classify and sequence material culture
   D. explain and delineate cultural processes

16. In general, there were three infrastructural conditions that led to the transformation of chiefdoms into the world's first states. Which of the following was NOT one of these?

   A. Circumscription
   B. Intensive agriculture
   C. Advanced weaponry
   D. Population increase

17. In kin terminology, the person of reference at the center of descent reckoning is referred to as the

   A. genotype
   B. phenotype
   C. genitor
   D. ego

18. Probably the most significant design feature of the human language is its ability to generate messages that have never been created before, and to make them intelligible to other speakers. This feature is described as language's

    A. openness
    B. semanticity
    C. patterning
    D. universality

19. A group that is defined by the patterns of interaction of its members is referred to as a

    A. society   B. tribe   C. race   D. culture

20. The main thought control device of pre-industrial states consisted – and still generally consists – of

    A. internalized sanctions
    B. magico-religious institutions
    C. externalized sanctions
    D. universal laws

21. Which of the following is not a trait or trend that separates hominids from other primates?

    A. Reduction of face, jaw, and anterior teeth
    B. Bipedalism
    C. Increased cranial capacity in Homo genus
    D. Prolonged infant dependency

22. As a population of species becomes more distanced from other populations, it undergoes gradual changes in traits and gene frequencies. These changes are known as

    A. alleles   B. clines   C. turns   D. mutations

23. The practice of defining territories on the basis of core features such as waterholes, watercourses, or landmarks is most typical of

    A. pastoralists
    B. industrialists
    C. food foragers
    D. horticulturists

24. In the archaeological record, the world's earliest known representative art was produced in the tradition known as

    A. Aurignacian
    B. Mousterian
    C. Oldowan
    D. Bronze Age

25. Of the following fossilized hominids, the Australopithecus _____ did NOT have an appreciable sagittal crest.

    A. aethiopicus
    B. boisei
    C. robustus
    D. afarensis

KEY (CORRECT ANSWERS)

1. A
2. A
3. B
4. D
5. C

6. D
7. D
8. A
9. B
10. B

11. D
12. C
13. D
14. B
15. C

16. C
17. D
18. A
19. A
20. B

21. D
22. B
23. C
24. A
25. D

TEST 5

DIRECTIONS: Each question or incomplete statement is followed by several suggested answers or completions. Select the one that BEST answers the question or completes the statement. *PRINT THE LETTER OF THE CORRECT ANSWER IN THE SPACE AT THE RIGHT.*

1. Which of the following, discovered at an archaeological site, would be an example of an ecofact?   1.____

   A. Patterned soil discolorations indicating rotted wood
   B. Pottery sherds
   C. Pollen
   D. Human remains

2. In communities where property is not to be allowed to threaten a more or less egalitarian social order, the use of _____ is used as a significant means of social maintenance.   2.____

   A. market exchanges   B. leveling mechanisms
   C. barter   D. balanced reciprocity

3. What is the term for a descent group composed of a number of supposedly related clans?   3.____

   A. Nucleus   B. Phratry   C. Pastor   D. Tribe

4. Anthropologist's predictions about the future are based on the scientific assumption that current trends will continue, that regularities observed in the past and present will also hold true in the future. This assumption is called   4.____

   A. homeostatic projection   B. occult prediction
   C. demographic transition   D. uniformitarianism

5. When a small part of one population migrates and takes with it a pool of genes that is not representative of its original group, _____ occurs.   5.____

   A. mutation   B. independent assortment
   C. the founder effect   D. gene flow

6. Which of the following is NOT a subfield of cultural anthropology?   6.____

   A. Paleoanthropology   B. Subsistence and economics
   C. Kinship   D. Worldview

7. The microlith is a tool type characteristic of the   7.____

   A. Lower Paleolithic   B. Middle Paleolithic
   C. Mesolithic   D. Neolithic

8. When a married couple takes up residence with either the husband's or wife's kin, this practice is known as   8.____

   A. neolocality   B. ambilocality
   C. ascription   D. uxorilocality

9. Which of the following is not a phase that is typically involved in a rite of passage?   9.____

   A. Separation   B. Veneration
   C. Incorporation   D. Margin

10. Which of the following is the best explanation for why early humans evidently formed permanent villages BEFORE domesticated varieties of grain were in use?
    The

    A. amount of labor and the heavy equipment needed to process wild grains required a more sedentary way of life
    B. aridity of the climate in most regions required a permanent settlement near an aquatic or marine food source
    C. lack of available game required fixed settlements near sites of wild grain and roots
    D. proliferation of domesticated animal food sources such as sheep and goats temporarily freed people from the need to develop agriculture

11. When a listener recognizes a spoken sound as having a certain linguistic function, he or she has recognized a

    A. phoneme   B. schema   C. phone   D. morpheme

12. The approach to human culture in which the human mind is viewed as the origin for the universal principles that order our behavior is

    A. behaviorism   B. structuralism
    C. uniformitarianism   D. functionalism

13. The subsistence pattern of pastoralism is an effective way of living in

    A. arid grasslands and deserts
    B. seasonal uplands
    C. temperate woodlands
    D. tropical wetlands

14. At the locus of an archaeological inquiry, which of the following terms is used to denote a distinctive occupation of the area by one specific group of people?

    A. Component   B. Stratus
    C. Assemblage   D. Site

15. The term *prognathic,* used in physical anthropology, refers to

    A. whether a hominid skull is robust or gracile
    B. the protrusion of facial features
    C. whether a species walked upright
    D. the bony ridge along the top of the skull

16. What is the term for the systematic, comparative study of patterns and processes in living and recent cultures?

    A. Ethnography   B. Ethnocentrism
    C. Ethnology   D. Ethnobiology

17. Each of the following statements about the descent group known as a clan is true EXCEPT

    A. they are usually exogamous
    B. membership is localized rather than dispersed
    C. they depend on symbols to provide members with solidarity
    D. members are unable to accurately trace their ancestry

18. Kin groups whose members assume descent from a common ancestor are referred to as

    A. tribes   B. castes   C. bands   D. clans

19. As chiefdoms made their transitions into the world's first states, they almost invariably underwent each of the following changes EXCEPT

    A. the elite could better support craft specialists and guards
    B. contributions to the central store became voluntary
    C. the redistribution of trade wealth and harvest surplus became more stratified
    D. there was less to be gained by leaving the society

20. The first stage of domestication for animals occurs

    A. when they are milked or slaughtered
    B. when they are first bred for certain traits
    C. when tame animals with genetically altered traits exist
    D. with the practice of animal husbandry

21. Determining the nature of dialectical relationships is a significant activity in the _____ view of human culture.

    A. holistic   B. reductionist
    C. materialist   D. idealistic

22. The habitat of a species, in addition to its lifestyle within that habitat, comprise the _____ of a species.

    A. biogram   B. niche   C. ego   D. role

23. Of the following events or situations, which is most likely to set the stage for a rite of intensification?

    A. Marriage   B. An approaching harvest
    C. Death   D. The onset of menses

24. The most powerful force for evolutionary change in any population arises from

    A. gene flow   B. mutation
    C. genetic drift   D. natural selection

25. *Dispersion and fission* is a stage of family evolution that begins when the

    A. first child is born   B. last child is born
    C. first child is married   D. last child is married

KEY (CORRECT ANSWERS)

1.	C	11.	A
2.	B	12.	B
3.	B	13.	A
4.	D	14.	A
5.	C	15.	B
6.	A	16.	C
7.	C	17.	B
8.	B	18.	D
9.	B	19.	B
10.	A	20.	D

21. A
22. B
23. B
24. D
25. C

42

EXAMINATION SECTION
TEST 1

DIRECTIONS: Each question or incomplete statement is followed by several suggested answers or completions. Select the one that BEST answers the question or completes the statement. *PRINT THE LETTER OF THE CORRECT ANSWER IN THE SPACE AT THE RIGHT.*

1. To pass judgment on how well one or another part of a society works, as compared against other societies, is acceptable social science procedure when done under the terms of

    A. ethnocentrism
    B. cultural relativism
    C. ethnoecology
    D. operational ecology

2. The mode of social group formation which offers MOST difficulty in permanently organizing society on a supra comnunity (multiple community) level is

    A. estate
    B. age-grade
    C. lineage
    D. class

3. The mode of social group formation which is MOST predictably present in any society that has only a minimal food-gathering technology is

    A. formal age-grade
    B. social class
    C. caste
    D. kinship

4. The factors which are constantly used as bases for organization of societies of all sizes and scale of complexity are

    A. kin and class
    B. kin and community
    C. community and rank
    D. rank and class

5. Among the following, the one which MOST predictably fosters inequality among the social sub-groups of a community is

    A. spinal-cord lineages
    B. men's clubs for community service
    C. statuses
    D. formal age-grades

6. The activity that illustrates purely the pattern of reciprocal exchange, as distinct from redistributive exchange is

    A. conducting funerals in Japan
    B. exchanging brass rods for a woman among the Tiv
    C. offering a potlatch on the Northwest Coast
    D. stealing a rival lesser-chief's wife among the Kiowa

7. Which of the following choices is definitely and clearly non-economic in nature?

    A. conducting funerals in Japan
    B. exchanging brass rods for a woman among the Tiv
    C. offering a potlatch on the Northwest Coast
    D. none of the above

8. In modern Japanese society as a whole, *inequality* is MOST explicity expressed in ranked

   A. estates   B. castes   C. statuses   D. clans

9. Which of the following are biologically established units that are recognized, whether socioculturally stressed or not, in any society?

   A. Nuclear families
   B. Age-grades
   C. Communities
   D. All of the above

10. In the ethnoecological view, New Guinea natives active in the Cargo Movement were making innovations *primarily* with respect to

    A. religion
    B. politics
    C. economics
    D. all of the above

11. In the operational ecological view, New Guinea natives, in establishing guarded squads to march to their fields, were making innovations *primarily* with respect to

    A. ideology
    B. social organization
    C. technology
    D. all of the above

12. Interpersonal relations within both traditional and modern Japanese families load GREATEST capacity for influence on other family members into the role of

    A. grandfather   B. father   C. mother   D. sister

13. In a patrilineal society, kin terminology is *likely* to

    A. equate mother and mother's brother
    B. equate father and father's brother
    C. differentiate all lineal relatives from all collateral relatives
    D. differentiate kin only by difference of generation

14. The expression $r = p - c - td$ symbolizes the

    A. market margin
    B. net return per unit area
    C. net return per mile of road
    D. none of these

15. Of the following, which relative turns out statistically to be most commonly preferred as a marriage partner in societies that express preference?

    A. Father's sister's daughter
    B. Father's brother's daughter
    C. Mother's sister's daughter
    D. Mother's brother's daughter

16. With reference to the Eskimo of North Alaska, it can be said that

    A. the two-part annual calendar of the Eskimo reflects their preoccupation with two periods, one of daylight and one of darkness
    B. new tools and weapons change culture rapidly

C. site characteristics always take precedence over situational characteristics
D. people residing in a harsh environment are more inventive than those residing in an easy environment

17. With reference to the domestication of corn, it can be said that

    A. the practice of corn popping antedates the cinema
    B. the "corn problem" centers around the presence of cobs but no kernels in explored caves
    C. wild corn is known as "corn pone"
    D. the term "corn ball" has been traced to the spherical patties of corn meal rolled out by the mentally retarded members of Aztec tribes as punishment for nose picking

18. The Eskimos' easy acceptance of death reflects

    A. their belief in the afterlife
    B. their weak family ties
    C. their feeling about their relationship to nature
    D. the power of their witch doctor

19. The technological development of the Australian Aborigines remained virtually unchanged until the 18th century. One of the MAJOR factors involved was the

    A. relative position of Australia with respect to other land masses
    B. physical environment of the continent
    C. racial composition of the Aborigines
    D. mental capacity of all primitive people

20. If a native dies and his brother marries the dead brother's wife, this is called

    A. incest   B. levirate   C. sororate   D. polygyny

QUESTIONS 21-23.

21. The diagram that respesents a patrilineal parallel cousin is

    A. I   B. II   C. III   D. IV

22. The nuclear (conjugal) family is represented in

    A. I   B. III   C. IV   D. V

23. The diagram that shows a matrilineal cross-cousin is

    A. II   B. III   C. IV   D. V

QUESTIONS 24-25.

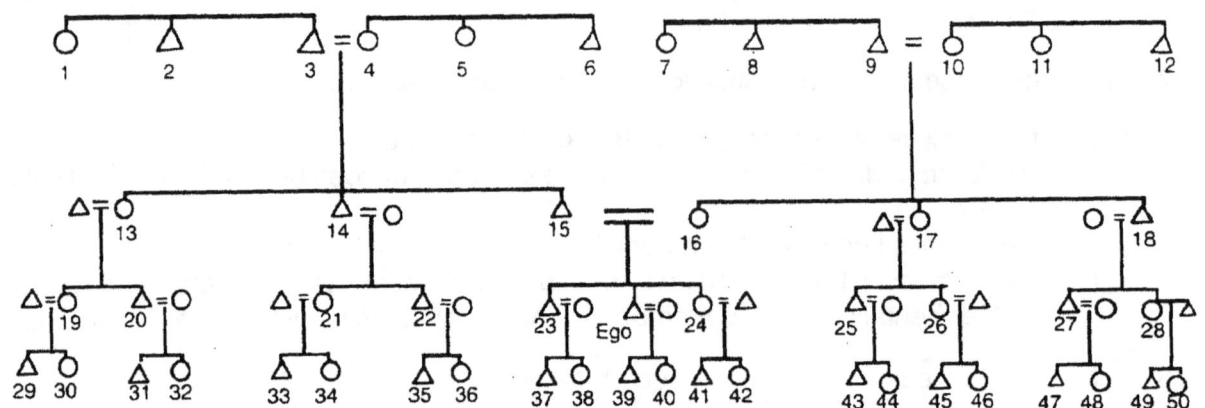

24. Ego's cross-cousins are

    A. 19, 20, 21, 22
    C. 19, 20, 27, 28
    B. 21, 22, 23, 24
    D. 25, 26, 27, 28

25. If Ego's society traces descent patrilineally, then the one who is NOT a member of Ego's mother's patrilineage is

    A. 11   B. 17   C. 27   D. 48

KEY (CORRECT ANSWERS)

1.	D	11.	B
2.	C	12.	A
3.	D	13.	B
4.	B	14.	B
5.	A	15.	D
6.	A	16.	B
7.	D	17.	A
8.	C	18.	C
9.	A	19.	A
10.	D	20.	B

21.	B
22.	C
23.	D
24.	C
25.	A

TEST 2

DIRECTIONS: Each question or incomplete statement is followed by several suggested answers or completions. Select the one that BEST answers the question or completes the statement. *PRINT THE LETTER OF THE CORRECT ANSWER IN THE SPACE AT THE RIGHT.*

1. In a lifetime, a person married once can belong to _____ clan(s). 1.____

    A. one
    B. two
    C. any number of
    D. five

2. In primitive societies, one would _____ expect to find a kinship system which provides just ONE term by which a person addresses all of his relatives. 2.____

    A. always   B. frequently   C. seldom   D. never

3. In any polygamous society, a census of conjugal families shows the MOST usual composition to be 3.____

    A. one husband, two or more wives
    B. one wife, two or more husbands
    C. two or more wives, two or more jusbands
    D. one wife, one husband

4. Members of a patrilineal spinal-cord lineage (NOT a household group) consist of males, and 4.____

    A. all their offspring
    B. their male offspring
    C. their wives, and all their offspring
    D. their wives, and their male offspring

5. Security is *greater* for a person under clan organization than under any type of family organization alone inasmuch as solidarity rests on the fact that fellow clansmen 5.____

    A. are all of the same demonstrated ancestry
    B. comprise a larger group than any family
    C. have no personal ties to his wife's (or husband's) relatives
    D. are all of the same sex

6. *Transhumance* means 6.____

    A. semiannual movements by pastoralists
    B. the use of irrigation systems
    C. slash-and-burn techniques of clearing land for farming
    D. farming based on root crops

7. The Eskimo adaptation to their environment includes 7.____

    A. a rigid and highly elaborated specialization and division of labor
    B. extreme hairiness
    C. a nomadic way of life in small family groups
    D. the absence of food-sharing

8. An ABSOLUTE dating technique is

   A. stratigraphy
   B. dendrochronology
   C. paleontology
   D. anthropometry

9. The widespread distribution of the complex ritual of the sun dance among Plains Indians can BEST be explained in terms of

   A. independent invention
   B. diffusion
   C. acculturation
   D. accidental juxtaposition

10. Man, as a primate, is characterized by

    A. warmbloodedness and live births
    B. stereoscopic vision and an opposable thumb
    C. bilateral symmetry
    D. all of the above

11. In reference to the economic and social basis of primitive bands, it can be said that

    A. the bands are considered to be primitive because there has been little evidence of concern for communal activities
    B. generally, bands whose livelihood is obtained by gathering are less primitive than those who hunt
    C. the population of a band and the area from which it derives its livelihood are a function of the number of people who customarily cooperate in economic and social activities at some time during the year
    D. the main characteristics which identify a primitive band include the complete absence of central authority, the pervading stigma attached to inter-family association, however minimal, and the lack of the concept of communal land ownership

12. In reference to horticulture and other subsistence techniques, it can be said that

    A. plants cannot be diffused without man's help
    B. in North America prior to the 15th century, horticulture contributed to the diet of at least 90% of the people
    C. food preserving processes came into use in North America only after settlement by Europeans
    D. The superabundance of animals in North America prior to its discovery by Columbus curtailed the development of specialized hunting instruments

13. In reference to the domestication of cattle, it can be said that

    A. cattle domestication was originally practiced only by nomadic peoples
    B. the sole motive for cattle domestication was to maintain the ready availability of a food supply
    C. the keeping of cattle for sacrificial purposes probably preceded their use as food
    D. the present-day sport of bull fighting can be considered an art-form representing the difficulties early man had in domesticating cattle

14. Hackenberg's comparative study of the Pima and Papago Indians supports the theory that

    A. an outstanding individual can change the direction of cultural development
    B. motivational patterns found among hunters and gatherers are incompatible with the introduction of modern agriculture
    C. hunters and gatherers adapt more readily than horti culturalists to modern agriculture because the former have a more flexible society
    D. two cultures utilizing marginal agricultural techniques may have different responses to agricultural innovations

15. The appearance of an organism is the sum of all its traits, and is known as the

    A. genotype   B. phenotype   C. species   D. evolution

16. In the first half of the twentieth century, some American anthropologists were concerned with delimiting geographical territories within which the cultures tended to be similar. These areas were known as

    A. boundaries   B. biomes
    C. cultural areas   D. homelands

17. Frequencies of genes in any given population may change because of
      I.   gene drift
      II. gene flow
      III. mutation
      IV. natural selection
    The CORRECT answer is:

    A. I only   B. I, II, IV
    C. II, III   D. All of the above

18. The changes which resulted from the introduction of monogamy into Tiwi society

    A. helped to perpetuate the traditional settlement pattern
    B. demonstrated the interrelatedness of all aspects of society
    C. demonstrated the value of the missionary's work
    D. allowed the Tiwi to live at a very high standard of living

19. MacNeish, in his article on Ancient Meso-American Civilization, demonstrates that for Tehuacan Valley, associated with each change in food production is a corresponding

    A. change in population, settlement, and social organization
    B. increase in the infant mortality rate
    C. decrease in the trade relations with other groups
    D. change in the social group involved

20. On the basis of the Von Thunen model, it may be stated that rent and transport costs are

    A. *inversely* related   B. *directly* related
    C. independent variables   D. none of these

21. According to the Von Thünen model, at any given distance from the market, the crop

    A. with the lowest transport rate is chosen
    B. for which there is the most market demand is chosen
    C. with the highest rent paying ability is chosen
    D. none of these

22. If the Von Thünen model is extrapolated to a world scale, the vegetable producing area near cities would be comparable to a(n)

    A. manufacturing region
    B. mining region
    C. area specializing in service functions (stock market, insurance sales, etc.)
    D. grazing area

23. If the Von Thünen model is extrapolated to a world scale, the empty zone beyond the farthest crop ring around a city would *most likely* be comparable to areas of

    A. the Soviet Bloc
    B. subsistence level tribal societies
    C. mining
    D. peasant societies

24. In his introduction to the section on "The Transition to Modernity," Cohen makes which of the following predictions about the society of the future?

    A. Biological criteria for determining inheritance of property will be replaced by social criteria of relationships
    B. The nuclear family will be replaced as the primary social unit in our society
    C. The rules of society will change so a man's worth is not based upon his productivity
    D. Man's life will eventually be controlled by his machines

25. Braidwood, in his article, "The Agricultural Revolution," argues that the

    A. agricultural revolution was a response to the great changes in climate which accompanied the retreat of the last glaciation
    B. isolation of man along with appropriate plants and animals in desert oases started the process of domestication
    C. agricultural revolution took place in forest lands which are still the home of simple agriculturalists
    D. agricultural revolution occured as the culmination of the ever-increasing cultural differentiation and specialization of human communities

KEY (CORRECT ANSWERS)

1. A
2. D
3. D
4. A
5. B

6. A
7. C
8. B
9. B
10. D

11. C
12. B
13. C
14. D
15. B

16. C
17. B
18. B
19. A
20. A

21. C
22. C
23. B
24. D
25. D

TEST 3

DIRECTIONS: Following is a passage that contains numbered blanks. Read the passage and answer the questions referring to each numbered blank that follow the passage.

PASSAGE

The history of western civilization is in large part measured by the history of western cities, particularly European cities. Early examples of these were the Greek city-states which often had their beginnings on or about a high, easily fortified point, such as the ___1___ in Athens. Populations of these city-states were small and democracy was a face-to-face practice. With the decline of the Greek city-states, Rome became ascendent. Besides the great central administrative centers, outposts or garrisons called ___2___ were located along the borders of the Empire. One such outpost was later to become the city of London. Within the metropolitan area of modern London is a special district called ___3___ which marks the site of the original Roman garrison camp.

With the decline of Rome, Europe was plunged into the Dark Ages from 500 to 1000 A.D. This was a time of urban decline when knowledge was kept alive in ___4___. Peasant/Lord relationships predominated and Feudalism was the mode of life. Little history is recorded for London at this time, but by the end of the first millenium, town building throughout Europe was renewed and London became a(n) ___5___, serving to concentrate shipments of wool from the island hinterland and to distribute goods particularly from the Netherlands and France. Little by little the importance of London grew, just as other cities on mainland Europe were increasing in size and wealth. The kings of England settled near the original Roman site of London at a place called Westminister and entered into a long feud with the merchants. This was exemplified when the famous Tower of London was built to dominate the city's defenses.

From 1500 to 1800, Europe experienced a period of relative stability. Cities grew slowly but steadily, and London become the mercantile center of a growing empire. With the industrial revolution, populations grew rapidly throughout western Europe and the size of the cities increased at an ever faster rate. At the present time, population growth is continuing and the cities are rapidly spreading geographically largely because of another revolution, one based on new and improved ___6___.

One classification of urban growth which relates to the types of technologies and materials employed has been suggested by ___7___. He speaks of a long-term "eotechnic" period of city growth which lasted from the time of the earliest towns until the Industrial Revoloution. The most common materials used for construction during this period were ___8___, and the major source of non-biotic energy was ___9___. This was also an era of handicraft manufacture with workers organized into guilds. It might be said that at this time labor and management were fused in a single entity.

The above period of urban growth was followed by another in the 19th century which is called the ___10___ period in this classification, Materials used for construction included iron. ___11___ was a major source of energy and the steam engine the most important energy converting device. Power was transferred from the steam engine to the various factory machines by belt drive mechanisms and vertical factories surrounded by workers' housing were the rule. Management dominated the production system, and low wages and long hours plus inefficient transportation systems meant that the workers had to live within walking distance of their jobs. Manufacturing areas were crowded and centrally located.

With the advent of the ___12___ period in the 20th century, the major source of energy has become hydrocarbon fuels while an important form of energy for manufacturing purposes is ___13___. Cheap and convenient individual means of transportation predominate, and workers and management vie with each other, or sometimes cooperate, thus making for a more equitable distribution of the products of manufacturing. Factories are usually only one story high, and the assembly line has become important.

Mobile middle-class workers, as well as management, have moved their residences to the suburbs, and factories seeking ___14___ land upon which to expand have also sought the outskirts of the cities. The workers' houses of the 19th century are now occupied by poorer migrants, and the high rents near the centers of cities as predicted by the ___15___ model of land use are provided by crowding of people into tenements. Thus, changes towards greater efficiency in production and transportation have nevertheless left urbanized areas of the western world with continuing problems which demand solution.

In the centuries that followed the domestication of grains and other crops, hunting and gathering rapidly diminished as sources of food. By 7000 B.C. food-producing communities appeared at lower elevations than the original wild habit of the potentially domesticable plants; that is, the growth of towns and cities occured at places other than the sites of the original farming communities. The period of "earliest civilization" (7000 to 5000 B.C.) as it is called by the archaeologist ___16___ was marked by its being the greatest single time of technological development until that of the period from Galileo through the Industrial Revolution. The four most important inventions dating from this period were ___17___.

This period of earliest civilization was followed by one of city growth sometimes referred to as the ___18___ Revolution. This was a time of further inventions and increasing administrative organization and was noted by the smelting of iron ore on a large scale, the building of aqueducts for the supplying of water to cities, and the invention of the ___19___ system and the ___19___ system. Thus, the stage was set for subsequent developments and for the long period of history leading to the Industrial Revolution. Meanwhile, it is important to keep in mind the possible different interpretations of Man's progress. Where one historian-archaeologist has emphasized the material development of Man, it may well be that the psychic development of Man as emphasized by the anthropologist ___20___ is even more important. Certainly this is a debate which will take many years to resolve, and which relates directly to the major struggle in the world today.

3 (#3)

1. A. Temple of Venus   B. Acropolis   1.___
    C. Mt. Olympus   D. Colosseum

2. A. fortresses   B. castles   C. castrum   D. rotundae   2.___

3. A. Little Rome   B. the Fort   C. Center Camp   D. The City   3.___

4. A. public schools   B. families   4.___
    C. universities   D. Christian monastaries

5. A. trade center   B. hub   5.___
    C. entrepot   D. large city

6. A. technology   B. religious fervor   6.___
    C. moral values   D. self-concepts

7. A. Von Thünen   B. Childe   C. Geddes   D. Redfield   7.___

8. A. aluminum   B. paper mache   8.___
    C. iron   D. wood and stone

9. A. water   B. milk   9.___
    C. plutonium   D. fruits and vegetables

10. A. neotechnic   B. paleotechnic   10.___
    C. zygotechnic   D. spherotechnic

11. A. coal   B. electricity   11.___
    C. hydraulic power   D. solar power

12. A. neotechnic   B. pyrotechnic   12.___
    C. hydrotechnic   D. solotechnic

13. A. solar power   B. fossil fuel   13.___
    C. electricity   D. natural gas

14. A. geographically desirable   B. low-rent   14.___
    C. high-risk   D. expensive

15. A. Geddes   B. Redfield   C. Childe   D. Von Thünen   15.___

16. A. Childe   B. Geddes   C. Redfield   D. Von Thünen   16.___

17. I. number system   II. wheel   17.___
    III. meal grinding   IV. fire
    V. solar calendar

    The CORRECT answer is:

    A. I, II, III, IV   B. I, II, III, V
    C. I, III, IV, V   D. II, III, IV, V

18. A. suburban   B. rural   C. urban   D. political   18.___

19. A. decimal, alphabet B. alphabet, roman numeral 19.____
    C. binary, judicial D. Judicial, alphabet

20. A. Geddes B. Childe C. Von Thünen D. Redfield 20.____

KEY (CORRECT ANSWERS)

1. B   11. A
2. C   12. A
3. D   13. C
4. D   14. B
5. C   15. D

6. A   16. A
7. C   17. B
8. D   18. C
9. A   19. A
10. B   20. D

TEST 4

DIRECTIONS: Following is a passage that contains numbered blanks. Read the passage and answer the questions referring to each numbered blank that follow the passage.

PASSAGE

Though it would be a mistake to think that hunting and gathering groups which survive today are the exact counterparts of all early men at the time when there was no knowledge of domesticated plants and animals, important information about resource using systems and social/spatial organization can be gained by studying these groups. The Eskimo are a good example of such a group. One example consists of a settlement of from three to five families (about thirty people at any one time). This society is a ___1___ one in which the father leads and controls the entire family group. In fact, the family is the highest social unit, and while camp leaders do develop, obedience to them is not mandatory. Neither is such leadership inherited. All property is shared, with the exception of ___2___. Any animal that is killed is shared by the whole group. Activities are restricted to a very few, of which ___3___ takes most of everyone's time. Everybody must do his share, and the careful designation of certain tasks as men's work or women's work is known as ___4___.

The survival of the Eskimo in a vast region having only limited resources is due in large part to their ability to store food, population control through infanticide and geronticide in extreme cases, and ___5___.

Although the Bushmen occupy a very different ecological setting, many of the general observations relating to the Eskimo hold true in their case as well. These people, who live in the ___6___ steppe/savannah region of South Africa are classified as hunters and gatherers. If their search for food were much more selective and specialized they might then be called hunters and ___7___. The Bushmen groups are somewhat larger than Eskimo groups, a condition probably resulting from a relatively greater abundance of game and other foods. The life of the Bushmen is adjusted to the climatic character of the region which can be described as having a ___8___ cycle. Because of these particular climatic conditions, the Bushmen usually camp near but not immediately beside ___9___. The hunting territory these people control is very large for the size of the group. They must move their camps several times each year and their equipment is limited not only by their restricted technical knowledge but also by lack of transportation.

The pattern of life of both the Eskimo and the Bushmen, as well as the Tiwi and other similar groups, has been described by the geographer ___10___ as constituting a biologic and ___11___ group which clusters about ___12___ at points of least transport, and which hold hunting and gathering territories for their exclusive use and which relocate as ___13___ as possible. Thus, although the details of these peoples' lives vary considerably, from the viewpoint of spatial organization their lives are quite similar.

The domestication of plants and animals by Man made a great difference in the number of people which can be supported in a given region. This important "revolution" in man's use of resources probably first took place in the Near East within the "Fertile Crescent" on the flanks of the ___14___ Mountains.

2 (#4)

Man's origins date back to at least 1,750,000 B.C. He is distinguished from the preceding, succession of two-legged, erect, man-like creatures referred to generally as __15__ by his use of tools. The period when Man first emerged and during which he learned, for example, to use and control fire is called the __16__. At the very end of this period Man made an important invention which has been suggested as an even better way to define at least "modern" man than the one mentioned above. This invention, not to be confused with domestications, was __17__.

The period of Man's history during which he domesticated plants and animals is called the __18__, and dates back in the Near East to at least 9,000 B.C. Remains from early settlement sites dating from this period include pieces of flint with a curious burnishing along their edges known as __19__. This burnishing seems to indicate that man at that time was already harvesting wild and/or domesticated grain-bearing grasses. By 8750 B.C. the primary farm village community had appeared. The pre-historian, Braidwood, in his article, "The Agricultural Revolution," describes the site where his excavations first uncovered the evidence cited above. This site is named __20__.

1. A. matriarchal   B. patriarchal   C. sororal   D. fraternal   1._____

2. I. weapons   II. food   III. rifles   IV. traps   2._____

    The CORRECT answer is:

    A. I, II   B. I, III, IV   C. II, III, IV   D. III, IV

3. A. food-gathering   B. praying   3._____
    C. fighting   D. singing

4. A. discrimination   B. contention   4._____
    C. allocation   D. tolerance

5. I.   religious beliefs and practices   5._____
    II. mobility
    III. excess body hair
    IV. adaptable diet
    V.   special hunting and fishing devices

    The CORRECT answer is:

    A. I, II, III   B. I, II, IV
    C. I, II, IV, V   D. II, III, IV, V

6. A. Sahara   B. Gobi   C. Negev   D. Kalahari   6._____

7. A. collectors   B. savers   C. sharers   D. explorers   7._____

8. A. variable   B. wet-dry   C. steady   D. arid   8. ____
9. A. animal dens   B. mountains   9. ____
    C. waterholes   D. sand dunes
10. A. Braidwood   B. Geddes   C. Redfield   D. Sauer   10. ____
11. A. cultural   B. triangular   C. geologic   D. exclusive   11. ____
12. A. ponds   B. trees   C. hearths   D. rivers   12. ____
13. A. quickly   B. frequently   C. quietly   D. infrequently   13. ____
14. A. Himalaya   B. Ural   C. Zagros   D. Pyrenee   14. ____
15. A. hominidae   B. arthropods   C. bipeds   D. mammalia   15. ____
16. A. Paleotechnic   B. Paleolithic   16. ____
    C. Neolithic   D. Neotechnic
17. A. the wheel   B. the pulley   C. matches   D. tools-making   17. ____
18. A. Neolithic   B. Geodesic   C. Geolithic   D. Paleolithic   18. ____
19. A. sickle-sheen   B. ferrous oxide   19. ____
    C. chromium   D. polishing by erosion
20. A. Olduvai Gorge   B. Jarmo   20. ____
    C. Lascaux   D. Sumer

KEY (CORRECT ANSWERS)

1. B   11. A
2. B   12. C
3. A   13. D
4. C   14. C
5. C   15. A

6. D   16. B
7. A   17. D
8. B   18. A
9. C   19. A
10. D   20. B

TEST 5

DIRECTIONS: Each question or incomplete statement is followed by several suggested answers or completions. Select the one that BEST answers the question or completes the statement. *PRINT THE LETTER OF THE CORRECT ANSWER IN THE SPACE AT THE RIGHT.*

1. The concept of adaptation is used by anthropologists to apply to

   A. both biological and cultural adaptation
   B. biological adaptation *only*
   C. cultural adaptation *only*
   D. primitive societies and industrial states
   E. technology but not to religion

2. The concept of culture as generally used by anthropologists would include

   A. technology and society but not ideology
   B. stone axes, marriage proposals and unicorns
   C. technology, society and ideology
   D. communism, fascism and democracy
   E. none of the above

3. Rules of exogamy

   A. are not found in cultures with rules of endogamy
   B. apply to sexual relations but not marriage
   C. establish alliances between groups through marriage
   D. are found in every known culture
   E. are found in some living non-human primate societies

4. In a culture with patrilineal clans, one would expect to find

   A. that Ego would marry his father's brother's daughter
   B. that Ego and his father's sister belong to the same clan
   C. that Ego would use the same kinship term for his sister and his mother's brother's daughter
   D. a matrilocal rule of post-marital residence
   E. a patrilocal rule of post-marital residence

5. The tribal level of organization is *generally* characterized by

   A. a permanent tribal leader
   B. mechanic solidarity
   C. social stratification
   D. social integration through both kinship and non-kinship associations
   E. a subsistence based upon hunting and gathering

6. Different cultures will establish themselves in stable co-existence in an area if

   A. they exploit different ecological niches
   B. they entered the area at the same time
   C. they receive about the same amount of military assistance from the modern industrial states

D. each group abhors the occupational activities of the other groups
E. the caste systems in the groups are compatible

7. The study of slash-and-burn agricultural societies demonstrates that

   A. poor soil productivity limits the cultural development of cultures with slash-and-burn agricultural technologies
   B. cultures with slash-and-burn agricultural technologies may develop toward civilizations where the area of usable land is limited
   C. civilization is the product of the genius of a people
   D. civilization is determined by cultural factors under specific conditions
   E. civilization is created by the vagaries of diffusion

8. The chiefdom level of organization is *usually* characterized by

   A. a hereditary position of chief
   B. a diversity of geographical environments within the area occupied by the chiefdom
   C. a redistribution of economic goods through the office of the chief
   D. unilineal descent groups with a major, or "royal," lineage
   E. differences in rank without social stratification

9. An archaeological site is excavated. It contains numerous potsherds and a number of postholes which apparently formed part of the walls of a structure 100 feet long. Within this long structure is a series of hearths.
   This site was *probably* occupied by a

   A. hunting and gathering band
   B. conjugal family
   C. hunting and foraging band
   D. joint family or localized lineage practicing agriculture
   E. patrilineage engaged in nomadic pastoralism

10. Which of the following BEST characterizes underdeveloped countries?

    A. Without assistance from industrial countries, they must develop by exploiting their own populations.
    B. Their lack of industrialization is due to their not having developed democratic forms of governments.
    C. They face the same problems the U.S. faced during its industrialization
    D. The industries they have are usually owned and controlled by modern industrial states.
    E. They have not industrialized because their populations lack the necessary motivations to improve their conditions.

11. An example of an early Neolithic village site would be

    A. Choukoutien   B. Sumer   C. Lascaux
    D. Olduvai Gorge   E. Jarmo

12. According to most anthropologists, warfare can be explained as

    A. the expression of primate aggression
    B. a necessary consequence of capitalism
    C. a means of males' expressing their masculinity

D. a type of cultural adaptation
E. a consequence of the old men of the society making the political decisions

13. Which of the following suggests that the men, at least, of hypothetical tribe X belong to recognized age-grade divisions?

    A. The tribe has major chiefs and lesser chiefs.
    B. Warriors live in separate residence-areas.
    C. They consider it undignified for mature and older men to hunt.
    D. A man's costume differs for a boy's costume.
    E. All persons undergo certain rites after a specified birthday.

14. Sharp's article, "Steel Axes for Stone Age Australians," illustrates the idea that

    A. the introduction of a new technological item may cause important changes in the society and ideology of a culture
    B. steel axes made possible a tribal level of development among the Yir Yoront
    C. the beliefs and meanings associated with an object may be just as important as its practical uses
    D. the technology of a culture may change while its society and ideology remain relatively stable
    E. a people may reject a new item of technology if it tends to destroy existing social relationships

15. The Australopithecines

    A. buried their dead
    B. are found throughout the Old World
    C. are the first upright, bipedal fossil hominids
    D. are classified as Homo erectus
    E. all of the above

16. Apes, monkeys, and the precursors of man share all of the following EXCEPT

    A. group sociability and year-round association of the sexes
    B. prolonged infant dependency
    C. protection of the females and their young by males
    D. territory
    E. symbolic vocal communications

17. On the basis of what we know about man's biological and cultural evolution, which of the following predictions are most likely to occur?
    I. The human species will not undergo any further biological modification.
    II. The various cultures in the world will converge toward a single, more homogeneous type.
    III. Technology will change at a faster rate than society.
    IV. The rate of gene flow among human populations will increase.
    V. The number of autonomous political units will decrease.

The CORRECT answer is:

    A. I, II   B. II, III   C. III, IV
    D. IV, V   E. III, V

18. Cross-cousins are Ego's
    I. mother's sister's children
    II. mother's brother's children
    III. father's brother's children
    IV. father's sister's children
    V. none of the above
    The CORRECT answer is:

    A. I, III
    B. II, IV
    C. III, V
    D. II, III
    E. IV, V

19. Trends in the general cultural evolution from the band to the industrial state are characterized by a (n)
    I. *decrease* in supernatural explanations for interpreting man's relation to nature
    II. *decrease* in sanctioned sexual relations outside of marriage
    III. *increase* in the amount of energy utilized by cultures
    IV. *increase* in the size of political units
    V. *decrease* in the importance of kinship as the basis for social organization
    The CORRECT answer is:

    A. I, II, III
    B. II, III, IV
    C. II, IV, V
    D. III, IV, V
    E. I, II, III, IV, V

20. The two doctrines, "all men are equal before the law," and "all men are naked before God," can be held with minimal conflict or mental compartmentalization by persons in a society based on the systems of inequality of
    I. caste
    II. class
    III. estate
    IV. ranked status
    V. ascription
    The CORRECT answer is:

    A. I, II
    B. II, III
    C. I, III
    D. II, IV
    E. IV, V

21. Which of the following is *most likely* the source of some of the major problems in the world today, according to anthropological consensus?
    I. Modern man has lost the basic human values characteristic of earlier periods of human history.
    II. The emphasis upon technology has made modern man more materialistic.
    III. Modern technology was developed as a means of destruction rather than for the benefit of mankind.
    IV. The populations of cultures have become too large for ffective administration
    V. The rate of technological change has been faster than the rate of change for society and ideology.
    The CORRECT answer is:

    A. I, II
    B. II, IV
    C. II, V
    D. III, IV
    E. IV, V

22. Referring to urbanization in West Africa, it has been found that
    I. urbanization inevitably leads to the alienation of he individual from his society
    II. voluntary associations are made up of and appeal primarily to the younger men
    III. voluntary associations promote the growth of civic loyalty and responsibility
    IV. women move to the urban centers as readily as men
    V. voluntary associations are an adaptation of African institutions to an urban environment
    The CORRECT answer is:

    A. I, II   B. I, III   C. II, III
    D. III, IV   E. IV, V

23. As a universal MINIMUM, mating and marriage are prohibited, as incestuous, between persons of which relationship to each other?
    I. Members of a single nuclear family
    II. Members of a single stem or extended family
    III. Persons of first cousin or closer relation
    IV. Persons of the same community
    V. Persons of any demonstrated kinship category
    The CORRECT answer is:

    A. I, II   B. I, III   C. II, IV
    D. III, V   E. IV, V

24. A cultural ecologist working in his own speciality accepts certain facts as "given" but should verify, evaluate and compare other facts for himself. Into which factors should he inquire for himself?
    I. Food-chains of plants and animals
    II. Soil and climate characteristics
    III. Relations with neighboring societies
    IV. World-view of the local population
    V. History of culture elements that are present
    The CORRECT answer is:

    A. I, II, III   B. II, III, IV   C. I, III, IV
    D. II, IV, V   E. III, IV, V

QUESTIONS 25-30. In each of the following sets, mark the lettered item that fits a numbered definition.

Set I

25. Marriage of a woman to her husband's brother
26. Property inheritance by the youngest child
27. Commoner estate among the Natchez Indians
28. Use-right granted by property (s) to someone else

A. levirate
B. agnate
C. sororate
D. ultimogeniture
E. none of these

Set II

29. Man who adopts female dress and social behavior, Plains Indians

30. Family type headed by female, without a permanently attached male

A. berdache
B. sororate
C. matricentral
D. couvade
E. none of these

29.____

30.____

KEY (CORRECT ANSWERS)

1. A	11. E	21. B
2. C	12. D	22. A
3. C	13. B	23. B
4. B	14. A	24. E
5. E	15. C	25. A
6. A	16. A	26. D
7. A	17. C	27. E
8. A	18. B	28. E
9. D	19. E	29. A
10. D	20. D	30. C

EXAMINATION SECTION
TEST 1

DIRECTIONS: Each question consists of a statement. You are to indicate whether the statement is TRUE (T) or FALSE (F). *PRINT THE LETTER OF THE CORRECT ANSWER IN THE SPACE AT THE RIGHT.*

1. In Greek, the terms "anthro" and "pology" refer respectively to "man" and "an apology for." 1.____

2. The view that the history of the world is a result of repeated and distinct creations is termed *cataclysm*. 2.____

3. Evolution is a movement towards simplicity. 3.____

4. A homeostat is a statistical principle. 4.____

5. Charles Darwin was the author of PRIMITIVE CULTURE. 5.____

6. Language is a system of conventional symbols. 6.____

7. All rules of polite behavior are identical, and are thus universal. 7.____

8. Cultural and linguistic diversity are attributed by anthropologists to inherited biological differences. 8.____

9. Culture may be viewed as the organism's way of adapting to its environment. 9.____

10. *Cultural primitivism* is caused by the primitive nature of the language spoken by the people. 10.____

11. Examples of instinctive human behavior, as opposed to cultural behavior, include such things as laughing, crying, gait, and sleeping positions, both in infants and adults. 11.____

12. Material culture and mechanical processes of technology are much more readily borrowed than ideas and abstract concepts. 12.____

13. Glottochronology is based on the premise that the basic vocabularies of a language change at a given rate. 13.____

14. Each culture includes within it the full range of potential human behavior patterns but chooses to emphasize only a few. 14.____

15. Insurance selling is a tertiary activity. 15.____

16. Manufacturing is a primary activity. 16.____

17. All settlements based upon mining are first order service centers. 17.____

18. If automobiles manufactured in the United States were sold *only* in the United States, their sale could NOT be described as basic to the country's economy in the "basic-non-basic" sense of the word. 18.____

19. Where transportation costs are concerned, brick kilns are to Coca Cola bottling works as penicillin is to wheat flour. 19.____

20. If three dairy farms are located 10, 100, and 1000 miles respectively from their market, one could expect fresh milk to be produced at the nearest, cheese produced at the second, and fresh butter produced at the farthest. 20.____

21. A person's peer group could be considered his family of orientation. 21.____

22. Society can be defined as an aggregate of organisms regulated by a certain set of conventions. 22.____

23. Evolution is a process of change. 23.____

24. A *cognate* is defined as a blood relative. 24.____

25. All the genes found in a population form a gene pool. 25.____

KEY (CORRECT ANSWERS)

1.	F	11.	T
2.	F	12.	T
3.	F	13.	T
4.	F	14.	T
5.	F	15.	T
6.	T	16.	F
7.	F	17.	T
8.	F	18.	T
9.	T	19.	F
10.	F	20.	F

21. F
22. T
23. T
24. T
25. T

TEST 2

DIRECTIONS: Each question consists of a statement. You are to indicate whether the statement is TRUE (T) or FALSE (F). *PRINT THE LETTER OF THE CORRECT ANSWER IN THE SPACE AT THE RIGHT.*

1. The SMALLEST unit of social organization is the tribe. 1.____

2. Barbers would *more likely* be found in all first order service centers than would gasoline stations. 2.____

3. As a general rule, the *higher* the level of technology of a group of people the *more* varied is the set of resources which they utilize. 3.____

4. Tools were invented in the Neolithic. 4.____

5. Plants were *probably* domesticated before animals. 5.____

6. All significant basic discoveries such as the smelting of iron ore on a large scale had been accomplished before the "Urban Revolution." 6.____

7. Initial city growth occurred in Central America concurrent with initial city growth in Mesopotamia. 7.____

8. Urbanization FIRST took place in the Selva regions of the world. 8.____

9. The original core areas of urbanization (e.g., Mesopotamia, Central America, etc.) all had similar environmental settings. 9.____

10. Spontaneous city growth is associated *only* with areas in the mainstream of Western Civilization. All other urban places are essentially "transplants" of Western culture. 10.____

11. Hierarchical ordering of space by human beings occurs *only* in western societies. 11.____

12. The accumulation of wealth, though not necessarily in the form of money, preceded city growth. 12.____

13. Although higher orders of central places incorporate lower order functions within themselves, a MAJOR exception to this rule is the general absence of agricultural production establishments in towns and cities. 13.____

14. One useful aspect of central place theory is its apparent cross-cultural applicability. 14.____

15. All societies retrace in their individual histories of development the general step-by-step developmental path of man as a modern, urban-dwelling species. 15.____

16. Population density is *directly* proportional to level-of-living (i.e., living standard). 16.____

17. Peasants are classified as "primitive cultivators." 17.____

18. In tribal societies production is *generally* limited to goods used by the producers. 18.____

19. Prebendal types of peasant domains are patrimonial. 19.____

20. The organization of a modern farm system more closely resembles that of a modern factory than it does that of a peasant village farm. 20.____

21. The number of customers needed for survival of an establishment determines the size of the area served and/or the number and type of services offered by a settlement. 21.____

22. "Central Place Theory" relates *only* to the location and NOT the size of settlements. 22.____

23. Generally speaking, hamlets in the United States are self-sufficient. 23.____

24. Central Places are service centers. 24.____

25. The highest order central place in the United States has been described as megalopolis. 25.____

KEY (CORRECT ANSWERS)

1. F	11. F
2. F	12. T
3. T	13. T
4. F	14. T
5. T	15. F
6. T	16. T
7. F	17. T
8. F	18. T
9. T	19. F
10. F	20. T

21. T
22. F
23. F
24. T
25. T

TEST 3

DIRECTIONS: Each question consists of a statement. You are to indicate whether the statement is TRUE (T) or FALSE (F). *PRINT THE LETTER OF THE CORRECT ANSWER IN THE SPACE AT THE RIGHT.*

1. All of the archaeological data at the Ishango site indicate that the two most important weapons, the spear and the harpoon, were invented elsewhere and diffused into this area. 1.____

2. The GREATEST prospect for the discovery of early sites, and hence the reconstruction of the chronology of early man in the New World, lies in the association of human settlements with marine and river terraces in Lower California and Texas. 2.____

3. The MOST outstanding difference between the Old and New World Neolithic revolutions is the large number of animals domesticated by the American Indians as opposed to the large number of plants domesticated in the Old World. 3.____

4. Considering the archaeological data found in the Valley of Tehuacan, it is better to describe the development of civilization in terms of a neolithic "evolution" rather than a neolithic "revolution." 4.____

5. "Slash and burn agriculture," as practiced in a Tropical Forest environment, is *incompatible* with permanent settlement. 5.____

6. Unlike humans, pre-human primates have no conception of territory and wander without restriction. 6.____

7. The pygmies living in the African rain forest are essentially serfs, and have no unique culture of their own. 7.____

8. Among the aborigines, the concept of territorial organization was not pervasive, and an individual had no political or legal ties to any particular system of organization. 8.____

9. When the Eskimo of North Alaska changed from a hunting and gathering to a trapping economy, less cooperation among the Eskimo resulted. 9.____

10. The domestication of animals was a prerequisite for the domestication of plants and sedentary farming. 10.____

11. In MOST primitive societies, premarital sexual activity serves as an intimate test of the compatibility of mating pairs before they actually enter into marriage, with all its social and economic responsibilities. 11.____

12. A general characteristic of early Neolithic communities appears to be specialization of production among workers. 12.____

13. An essential difference between a lineage and a clan is that members of a lineage can actually trace out their geneologies of common descent from a known ancestor, while clan members cannot. 13.____

14. The concept of adaptation can refer to both synchronic and diachronic phenomena- that is, it refers to the process of modification to selective pressures as well as how an organism or population is organized in relation to its environment at a particular time. 14.____

15. Ethnoscience is an attempt to get at the way people classify things and is therefore always concerned with the cognized environment. 15.____

16. A BASIC limitation of kinship as an organizing principle is that it is limited by biology-that is, the fact that kinship is directly tied in with biological factors prevents it from organizing large numbers of people. 16.____

17. The fact that until sixty years ago the forest products used in the Northeast United States came from the Great Lakes area rather than the Pacific Northwest is an example of transferability. 17.____

18. Improvement in transportation has produced two contrasting and contradictory results: (1) increased similarities between areas, and (2) specialization within areas. 18.____

19. Berry and Garrison endeavored to prove statistically that based on the number of functions performed and on groups of functions, a hierarchy of central places exists. 19.____

20. Deevey, in his article on "Human Population," states that cannibalism is the MOST rational voluntary control over population numbers. 20.____

21. An example of gene flow can be found in populations that inbreed. 21.____

22. Natural selection is a term used to describe the survival of those organisms MOST suited for their environment. 22.____

23. Mutation is a freak, temporary change in the genetic makeup of an organism, and CANNOT be passed on to future generations. 23.____

24. Dominance hierarchies provide order in a society by letting each individual realize his role and function in the society. 24.____

25. An epideictic display informs members of the society about the size and density of that society, BEFORE members take any action to change that size or density. 25.____

KEY (CORRECT ANSWERS)

1. F
2. T
3. F
4. T
5. F

6. F
7. F
8. F
9. T
10. F

11. T
12. F
13. T
14. T
15. F

16. T
17. F
18. F
19. T
20. T

21. F
22. T
23. F
24. T
25. T

TEST 4

DIRECTIONS: Each question consists of a statement. You are to indicate whether the statement is TRUE (T) or FALSE (F). *PRINT THE LETTER OF THE CORRECT ANSWER IN THE SPACE AT THE RIGHT.*

1. The domestication of maize in the New World occured at *approximately* the same date as that of wheat in the Fertile Crescent. 1.____

2. Maize was the *only* plant crop domesticated in the New World. 2.____

3. Only a few places and/or ethnic groups in North America produced a surplus of food. 3.____

4. High Indian population densities in North America were in all cases *directly* related to the availability of domesticated plants. 4.____

5. Spanish occupation of portions of North America preceded occupation by North Europeans by at least 100 years. 5.____

6. The pattern of agricultural resource use introduced by English settlers was everywhere the SAME in North America. 6.____

7. The MAJOR waves of European immigration to North America began about 200 years after the first North European invasion of the continent. 7.____

8. While the Indian occupation of North America showed a direct adjustment to resource availability, no such correlation existed for the locating of North European settlers. 8.____

9. World population growth during the Historic Period was slow until recently, but homogeneous in space and through time. 9.____

10. Pre-industrial societies were typified by high birth and low death rates. 10.____

11. Pre-industrial societies were typified by life expectancies: of less than 30 years. 11.____

12. "Developed" societies are in theory typified by low birth and death rates. 12.____

13. World population is at present typified by high birth and low death rates. 13.____

14. The population of Europe from 1650 to the present has maintained *approximately* the SAME percentage share of total world population. 14.____

15. Africa's population in proportion to the total world population has rapidly *increased* its percentage share of the total in the last 300 years. 15.____

16. A chicken is an egg's way of reproducing another egg. 16.____

QUESTIONS 17-25.

DIRECTIONS: Each question or incomplete statement is followed by several suggested answers or completions. Select the one that BEST answers the question or completes the statement. *PRINT THE LETTER OF THE CORRECT ANSWER IN THE SPACE AT THE RIGHT.*

17. The Middle East village

    A. is an important economic unit in that it performs break-in-bulk functions for agricultural products raised by dispersed clusters of nomads
    B. supplies larger urban concentration and nomadic camps with cereals and other vegetable foodstuffs
    C. can be considered a low order central place devoted to the manufacture of goods needed by its tributary population
    D. is located according to factors of situation, rather than of site

18. The statement which is TRUE is:

    A. The rise of towns and cities during the late Neolithic period has been attributed to nearly optimum agricultural conditions and a social organization in which certain groups had control over agricultural surplus.
    B. The countries in which the Industrial Revolution first began now lead all other countries in the rate of unbanization.
    C. In cities, the increase of the number of people and their density per unit of land area consistently go hand-in-hand.
    D. Urban growth in "underdeveloped" countries is not related to the amount of contact they have with "developed" countries.

19. The statement which is TRUE is:

    A. In Mesopotamia, Central America, and South Asia, concern with fortification accompanied urban development.
    B. Irrigated agriculture together with the centralized control needed to build and maintain irrigation works were two factors which contributed to urban development in Mesopotamia.
    C. Early cities lacked a dominant focal center.
    D. There are few characteristics which differentiate the early city from a village-farming community.

20. The TRUE statement regarding population is:

    A. The population curve has moved upward in steps corresponding to the great "revolutions" of history.
    B. The only check on population size is the nature of the environment.
    C. There is strong evidence in support of the argument that longevity and population density are related.
    D. None of the above.

21. Reasons for the development of two basically different types of cities in Western Europe, as opposed to traditional China, would include:

    A. Physically, China lacked Europe's outstanding advantages for trade.
    B. Europe was politically more stable than China since it possessed a long period of continuous central authority.
    C. European merchants did not use their money to establish their independence as did merchants of Canton and Shanghai.
    D. In Europe, with the preponderant position of agriculture, merchants never occupied proportionately as large a place in the economy.

22. In an industrial, as opposed to a pre-industrial city, you do NOT find

   A. extra-community economic organization in which recruitment is based more upon universalism than on particularism
   B. a small and flexible kinship system
   C. mass communication
   D. a class system which stresses ascription rather than achievement

23. A system explaining material interaction can be based on

   A. complimentarity, intervening opportunity, spatial hierarchy
   B. discontinuity, intervening opportunity, isolated states
   C. complimentarity, intervening opportunity, transferability
   D. central place theory, space packing, transferability

24. Within the Middle East the location of the village is dependent on

   A. arable land   B. elevation
   C. water   D. transportation facilities

25. If Ego dies and his brother marries Ego's wife (i.e., replaces Ego), this is called

   A. incest   B. levirate   C. sororate   D. polygyny

KEY (CORRECT ANSWERS)

1.	F	11.	T
2.	F	12.	T
3.	T	13.	T
4.	F	14.	T
5.	T	15.	F
6.	F	16.	T
7.	T	17.	D
8.	F	18.	A
9.	F	19.	B
10.	F	20.	A

21. A
22. B
23. C
24. C
25. B

TEST 5

DIRECTIONS: Each question consists of a statement. You are to indicate whether the statement is TRUE (T) or FALSE (F). *PRINT THE LETTER OF THE CORRECT ANSWER IN THE SPACE AT THE RIGHT.*

1. All neolithic cultures were directly or indirectly derived from the Near East, where plants and animals were first domesticated. 1.____

2. It can be argued that apes have culture because they live in societies. 2.____

3. Ethnocentrism is a subdivision of anthropology. 3.____

4. Cave paintings first appear in the Upper Paleolithic. 4.____

5. Expansion of the brain in early hominid evolution was a consequence of tool using and bipedal locomotion. 5.____

6. Present-day variation between populations or "races" is BEST explained by the mechanisms of mutation, selection, genetic drift and migration. 6.____

7. Genetic drift is the process by which genes move from one population to another. 7.____

8. Peking Man and Java Man are both classified as Homo erectus. 8.____

9. According to Hoebel, Neanderthal is to be understood as a distinctive, specialized cold-climate sub-species of Homo sapiens, derived from the same Homo sapiens base as modern man. 9.____

10. The Chinese writing system can be said to have gone beyond pictography, but still falls short of pure phonetic representation. 10.____

11. Both L.H. Morgan and E. Tylor viewed cultural evolution as progressive. 11.____

12. Boas and the American School saw cultures as made up of a number of traits. 12.____

13. According to R. Benedict, configurations are to culture as personality is to the individual. 13.____

14. Kroeber and Sapir were interested in the question of the function of culture, rather than its nature. 14.____

15. Cultural primitivism is caused by the primitive nature of the language spoken by the people. 15.____

16. Grocery stores would be *more likely* to be found in all first order service centers than would barbers. 16.____

17. Chisholm mentions that Von Thünen introduced a series of modifications into his agricultural model, after the primary variables had been identified. However, Von Thünen did NOT modify his assumption of the single isolated market. 17.____

18. Von Thünen's theory of land use is based on his calculation of the Economic Rent accruing to each type of land use at various distances from the central city. 18.____

19. Brush states that many geographers are unwilling to accept the theories that have developed about trade centers because these theories assume a perfectly uniform territory.   19._____

20. It is Brush's belief that the locational pattern of trade centers was controlled *mainly* by the radial movement of traffic which creates circular trade areas and the equidistant spacing of centers.   20._____

21. A significant unifying factor in the last half of the nineteenth century was the introduction of Darwin's Theory of Evolution and the concept of genetics.   21._____

22. An *affine* is defined as a blood relative.   22._____

23. Progress and evolution are *always* synonyms.   23._____

24. Gene frequencies can be changed by gene flow, genetic drift, mutation, and natural selection.   24._____

25. Man is supposed to have 25 sets of chromosomes.   25._____

KEY (CORRECT ANSWERS)

1.	F	11.	T
2.	T	12.	T
3.	F	13.	T
4.	T	14.	F
5.	T	15.	F
6.	T	16.	T
7.	F	17.	T
8.	T	18.	T
9.	T	19.	T
10.	T	20.	T

21.	T
22.	F
23.	F
24.	T
25.	F

EXAMINATION SECTION
TEST 1

DIRECTIONS: Each question or incomplete statement is followed by several suggested answers or completions. Select the one that BEST answers the question or completes the statement. *PRINT THE LETTER OF THE CORRECT ANSWER IN THE SPACE AT THE RIGHT.*

1. In the Kalahari Desert, we find today the survivors of a once-numerous race of primitive food gatherers who are entirely without agriculture. They are

    A. Zunis B. Ainus C. Neanderthals
    D. Watusis E. Bushmen

2. A group resulting from descent reckoned either from the father's or mother's line is called

    A. ethnological B. patriarchal C. matriarchal
    D. lineage E. primitive

3. A culture marked by a subsistence technique centered about the herding and husbandry of domesticated animals is called

    A. riparianism B. humanism C. naturalism
    D. chauvinism E. pastoralism

4. _____ comprehends both rights and duties. It is an individual's comparative prestige rank in a community.

    A. Status B. Caste C. Lineage
    D. Stratum E. Stasis

5. The totality of biological traits transmitted by the parents and determining the individual's capacity for growth and development is his

    A. hereditament B. chromosome C. heredity
    D. congenitalism E. environment

6. Primates, including all forms of man, extinct and living, are or were

    A. homo sapiens B. hominoids C. homophiles
    D. higher apes E. four-legged

7. The custom of requiring or permitting a man to marry the widow of his brother is

    A. widespread in the United States and France
    B. an outgrowth of human slavery and feudal serfdom
    C. called levirate
    D. the American way of death
    E. imbedded in mortality tables

8. A crowd is well known to be emotional, irrational, and violative of human rights. Pure democracy

    A. is always handicapped by inertia
    B. is the American form of government
    C. invariably protects minority rights

D. will show the same traits
E. is distinguished by tolerance of dissent

9. Cooley has said, *A mechanic can more easily keep the habit of simple look and speech since he does not have to learn to conceal his thoughts to the same degree that the lawyer and merchant do.*
   This idea may be rephrased as follows:

   A. One picture is worth a thousand words
   B. The pen is mightier than the sword
   C. Blessed are the meek, for they shall inherit the earth
   D. It is better to have the hand subdued to what it works in than the soul
   E. Oh, what a tangled web we weave, when first we practise to deceive!

10. In the professions, there is, as a rule, no definite measure of charge for services; and, consequently, professional men tend to base their charges on their view of what the client will pay, thus

    A. giving to each according to his needs and taking from each according to his ability
    B. inevitably providing socialization of the professions
    C. inviting government price control
    D. reducing their total income
    E. accustoming themselves to exploit the wealth or weakness of others

11. Many, if not most, businessmen regard their occupations as a form of _____ rather than as a form of service.

    A. hobby   B. joke   C. game
    D. war   E. therapy

12. Sociology, in a broad, general sense, can be defined as

    A. the study of neurosis and its effects on groups
    B. the study of the individual in relation to his employment
    C. the study of the effect of environment on man
    D. an inquiry into man in relation to his time
    E. the study of human beings in their group relationships

13. Sociologists are more interested in the _____ rather than in the _____ in their researches.

    A. recurrent; unusual
    B. statistical; philosophical
    C. dynamics of group; patterns of behavior
    D. whole community; small minority
    E. problems of married couples; problems of the individual

14. There are those who, because of their disbelief in the concept of _____ insist that there can be no science of human behavior.

    A. identical units   B. psychoanalytical theory
    C. experimental method   D. objective method
    E. empirical knowledge

15. Culture can BEST be defined as the
    A. arts and humanities of a society
    B. way of living which a society develops to meet its fundamental needs
    C. style of conversation and manners of a society
    D. uniqueness of a society's contributions to the life of its times
    E. religious and moral attitudes of a society as expressed in the arts

16. _____ is the process by which culture is passed on to each succeeding generation through learning.
    A. Cultural transmission   B. Osmosis
    C. Reading   D. Group pride
    E. Cultural accumulation

17. Culture is limited MOSTLY by
    A. man's biological needs and capabilities
    B. man's religious beliefs
    C. man's inability to adjust
    D. anti-intellectual groups
    E. mediocre artisans

18. The Mediterranean race is a part of the _____ race.
    A. Caucasian   B. Mongoloid   C. Negroid
    D. Australoid   E. Alpine

19. Which of the following is MOST frequently used in establishing racial groupings?
    A. Cephalic index   B. Culture
    C. Language   D. Folk songs and tales
    E. Intelligence quotients

20. Which of the following races is rated superior by sociological standards?
    A. Mongoloid   B. Caucasian   C. Negroid
    D. Australoid   E. None of the above

21. The SIMPLEST unit of a culture is
    A. trait   B. structure   C. family
    D. youth   E. religion

22. Cultural change originates from
    A. revolution   B. invention
    C. philosophy   D. group migration
    E. new artists

23. Ethnocentrism arises when a group
    A. departs from its environment
    B. fears attack
    C. intermarries
    D. feels superior culturally
    E. feels inferior

24. Cultural change is

    A. impossible
    B. difficult
    C. destructive
    D. superficial
    E. universal

25. Sociologists use the term *diffusion of culture* when referring to the

    A. cultural differences among groups
    B. dissolution of a culture
    C. spreading of cultural traits or complexes from one society to another
    D. gradual disbelief in culture by a society
    E. changing of culture to meet the new needs of a society

26. When a culture borrows a new trait from some other culture, it USUALLY

    A. reacts hostilely
    B. changes old traits to fit the new trait
    C. modifies the trait to fit its practices and beliefs
    D. seeks the advice of group elders
    E. makes it a religious principle

27. Not all inventions are accepted and put into use even by the society within which they originate. There are many and compelling reasons for this.
    One of these is NOT a reason:

    A. The culture may not have progressed to a degree where the invention can be put to use
    B. The new invention or trait, however practical, may cause a disruption
    C. Ideological reasons for not using the invention may be stronger than the group's need for it
    D. The individuals in the society may not feel a need for what the new trait or invention can offer
    E. Culture tries to separate itself from what may appear in vogue since it has greater need for tradition

28. A social system can BEST be described as

    A. the organization of reciprocal rights and duties which the culture prescribes for people occupying various positions in the society
    B. the part the monarch, president, or other leaders play in the granting of favors to certain groups within the culture
    C. the morals that guide individuals in their behavior patterns
    D. the attitudes of individuals toward one another and toward groups in their social order
    E. none of the above

29. The process by which members of various groups come to participate in specific parts of the culture while occupying different positions in society is known as

    A. social differentiation
    B. Parkinson's law
    C. functionalism
    D. prejudice
    E. orientation

30. _____ consists of the rights and duties assigned to a person on the basis of his participation in one aspect or another of the culture.

    A. Personality aggregation
    B. Group dynamics
    C. Social caste
    D. Status
    E. Racial superiority

31. All medicine men, all lawyers, all clergymen presumably behave according to a specified pattern termed

    A. sexual identity
    B. moral attitudes
    C. cultural roles
    D. marital status
    E. traits

32. An established way of doing something which is recognized by the society as the *correct* way of doing it is a

    A. custom
    B. ritual
    C. positive reaction
    D. conformity
    E. non-creative act

33. Which of the following characteristics is UNTRUE of rural populations?

    A. Large families
    B. More intimate knowledge of neighbors
    C. Gossip influencing behavior of individuals
    D. Greater emphasis on geographic proximity as a basis for group association
    E. Little emphasis on making the family an economic unit of production

34. Which of the following is NOT among the psychological characteristics attributed to American farmers by T. Lynn Smith?

    A. Conservative and orthodox
    B. Thrifty and frugal
    C. Fatalistic and resigned
    D. Suspicious and observant
    E. Especially bizarre sexual behavior and practice

35. Agricultural and _____ are the two principal types of villages.

    A. urban
    B. exurban
    C. suburban
    D. Utopian
    E. industrial

36. _____ is NOT a characteristic peculiar to urban life.

    A. Emphasis on secondary groups
    B. Anonymity
    C. Relatively heterogeneous population
    D. Social mobility
    E. Discrimination

37. The coordinations of the nervous and muscular systems are incomplete

    A. in primitive man
    B. without civilization
    C. throughout life, depending on the individual

D. at birth
E. until puberty

38. Man differs from all other animals in his larger brain and his ability to 38.____

   A. walk on two legs   B. talk
   C. learn   D. recall
   E. adapt to environment

39. A child reared in isolation will NOT naturally 39.____

   A. eat
   B. sleep
   C. talk
   D. take shelter
   E. investigate his surroundings

40. If a child is reared by a wolf, he will act and behave 40.____

   A. like primitive man
   B. exactly like a wolf
   C. like a younger child
   D. just like other children of his age
   E. as nearly like a wolf as his anatomy will permit

41. Though man's learning capacity is great, the heredity of his species sets limits. 41.____
    He cannot

   A. acclimate himself to extremes of hot or cold
   B. swim under water
   C. live in isolation
   D. hear the ticking of a watch at 40 feet
   E. join a primitive tribe and live according to its customs

42. One of the ways of changing the quality of an animal species is by 42.____

   A. education   B. breeding   C. birth control
   D. reproduction   E. insemination

43. Riesman's depiction of modern man as *other-directed* in contrast to *tradition-directed* 43.____
    and *inner-directed* leads to the widely-held view that modern man

   A. evaluates success in terms of the wealth he is able to amass
   B. evaluates success in terms of the approval of his peers
   C. is much too altruistic
   D. tends to discard all tradition regardless of its value
   E. regards other people as of relatively greater worth than himself

44. *Argot* is 44.____

   A. a form of political phraseology
   B. the language used by now-obsolete tribes
   C. a caveat
   D. the slang of a group
   E. the conventional usage of the English language

45. Social forces may be inclusively defined as those factors arising in the _____ environment. 45.____

    A. natural   B. human   C. religious
    D. political   E. terrestrial

46. The family institution is essentially a(n) _____ relationship. 46.____

    A. mother-child   B. pathological C. outmoded
    D. father-son   E. incestuous

47. An hereditary and endogamous class of persons is known as a(n) 47.____

    A. potlatch   B. urban society
    C. social institution   D. shaman
    E. caste

48. The disposition to live in aggregations and to move in masses is called 48.____

    A. anthropomorphism   B. isolation
    C. evolution   D. gregariousness
    E. society

49. A process by which an individual or social unit tries to be like, or act like, some model or example is termed 49.____

    A. association   B. deviation   C. imitation
    D. derivation   E. acceptance

50. The languages of primitive people are _____ in structure. 50.____

    A. very simple   B. highly complex   C. anarchic
    D. archaic   E. anachronistic

KEY (CORRECT ANSWERS)

1. E	11. C	21. A	31. C	41. D
2. D	12. E	22. B	32. A	42. B
3. E	13. A	23. D	33. E	43. B
4. A	14. A	24. E	34. E	44. D
5. C	15. B	25. C	35. E	45. B
6. B	16. A	26. C	36. E	46. A
7. C	17. A	27. E	37. D	47. E
8. D	18. A	28. A	38. B	48. D
9. D	19. A	29. A	39. C	49. C
10. E	20. E	30. D	40. E	50. B

TEST 2

DIRECTIONS: Each question or incomplete statement is followed by several suggested answers or completions. Select the one that BEST answers the question or completes the statement. *PRINT THE LETTER OF THE CORRECT ANSWER IN THE SPACE AT THE RIGHT.*

1. American children are becoming taller than their parents. This increase in size is probably due to

    A. nuclear fallout
    B. selection of the fittest
    C. the mating of larger people
    D. the processes of evolution and devolution
    E. better feeding and a decline in disease

2. Shutting the door on travelers is almost unknown among

    A. Southerners   B. preliterate cultures
    C. urbanites   D. small businessmen
    E. American farmers

3. In all social systems, members are classified on the basis of _____ and _____. These classifications serve as prerequisites for all other classifications in the society.

    A. education; income   B. height; weight
    C. health; education   D. age; sex
    E. wealth; talent

4. Aggression among the lower classes in our culture generally takes the form of

    A. striving for greater income
    B. competition
    C. aspiring to better education
    D. fighting
    E. rape

5. Among primitive peoples, _____ plays the LEAST important part in determining cultural roles.

    A. sex   B. ability   C. strength
    D. occupation   E. age

6. The ULTIMATE power of any government is, of necessity,

    A. coercive   B. permissive   C. consensual
    D. dictatorial   E. to be tolerated

7. All human societies have some concept of the supernatural. The PRINCIPAL function of religion is usually to

    A. orient man with respect to the supernatural
    B. counteract this concept
    C. make man fearful of the supernatural
    D. make man unafraid of the supernatural
    E. create a clerical hierarchy

8. This _____ is a person recognized by many primitive peoples to have a special relationship with the supernatural.

   A. shabbas B. shamus C. shaman
   D. shalom E. shadrach

   8._____

9. The Social Darwinists believed that _____ was inevitable.

   A. the process of conflict B. religious intermarriage
   C. miscegenation D. nuclear war
   E. polygamy

   9._____

10. A PRINCIPAL object of any society is to effect

    A. social control
    B. unquestioning obedience
    C. complete personal freedom
    D. ecumenism
    E. separation of church and state

    10._____

11. Man can digest only certain foods and does not eat grass, for example. But whether or not a group of people will eat, for instance, cows or pigs is

    A. culturally determined
    B. biologically determined
    C. a matter of individual differences
    D. always determined by religion
    E. never determined by religion

    11._____

12. A marriage can be polygamous or monogamous and still

    A. legally exist in the United States
    B. find sanction in every culture
    C. result in reproduction
    D. be a product of a homosexual alliance
    E. be celebrated in a Catholic church

    12._____

13. The theory that everyone's needs are satisfied by self-interest alone is related by modern sociologists with

    A. the Rand School B. the Spencerian fallacy
    C. *greed, not need* D. Christianity
    E. Jeffersonian democracy

    13._____

14. Culture may be defined as

    A. a society's learned and shared ways of behaving
    B. the basis of a society
    C. the absorption of a society's history
    D. the folklore of a society
    E. the study of atypical individual in a society

    14._____

15. Mores, according to Sumner, differ from folkways in that

    A. they are unchanging and universal
    B. they are religious in basis

    15._____

C. they result from a society's defense structure
D. breaking them is considered a threat to a society's welfare, while violation of folkways can often occur with relative impunity
E. the more different they appear, the more they are the same

16. Prescribed patterns of conduct which have the authority of, and are enforced by, the state are

    A. conventions B. customs C. mores
    D. folkways E. laws

17. Odum and his followers use the term *technicways* to characterize one of the following descriptions:

    A. Rapid technological adjustments which arise through the incidence of new techniques and inventions, and their use in social life
    B. The ways of group manipulation
    C. The slow triumph of technology over man
    D. The need of certain men to sublimate by submitting themselves to technology rather than adapting it to meet their needs
    E. The New Industrial Revolution

18. Large aggregations of human beings living close together increase GREATLY the chances of

    A. tyranny
    B. spreading contagious and infectious diseases
    C. homogeneity
    D. homosexuality
    E. suicidal tendencies

19. In rural areas, the actions of an individual are MORE likely to be

    A. conforming B. prying C. imitated
    D. observed E. insipid

20. Human ecology is the study of the adaptation of men to

    A. new ideas B. other men C. environment
    D. women E. alien cultures

21. In primitive times, the absence of money was naturally accompanied by

    A. frequent outbreaks of hostilities among neighboring tribes
    B. a lack of educational facilities
    C. an increase in trade among nations
    D. perpetual poverty
    E. systems of gifts and barter

22. Socialists call the driving force which puts all the machinery of capitalism in motion the

    A. power structure B. profit motive
    C. opiate of the people D. delusion of the masses
    E. establishment

23. When purchasing power increases more rapidly than production, _____ results.

    A. depression B. prosperity C. fascism
    D. socialism   E. capitalism

24. Regulation by government of economic agencies in modern society has been MAINLY concerned with

    A. ethics   B. education   C. social work
    D. public health E. public utilities

25. Such peoples as the Andaman Islanders and the Australian Bushmen have no specially constituted government, as may be seen from the fact that they have

    A. chieftains
    B. missionaries in their midst
    C. no formal rulers
    D. no written language
    E. many primitive rituals

26. The boat of the Vikings became the major instrument of aggression all along the western coast of Europe as, in the same era, did _____ in the borderland between Asia and Europe.

    A. the horse   B. gunpowder
    C. the camel   D. the Mongols
    E. the Visigoths

27. Where one primitive group is superior in the manufacture and possession of utilitarian tools to a neighboring group, there is commonly a tendency to

    A. sell or barter unfairly
    B. assume future superiority
    C. wage war
    D. exchange materials for knowledge and/or work techniques
    E. fall behind culturally

28. War between groups is an organized activity that is

    A. instinctive
    B. the forerunner of progress and change
    C. necessary to be learned
    D. invariably the result of individual differences
    E. ultimately beneficial to both groups

29. Malinowski has defined war as the use of organized force between two politically independent units in pursuit of

    A. freedom   B. wealth   C. territory
    D. a better society E. tribal policy

30. A *state* is created by the development of the function of _____ in a given community.

    A. encouraging dissension   B. stimulating individuality
    C. maintaining order   D. nullification
    E. decentralization

31. Burke stated, with regard to the representative republic, that the common man is a(n)   31.____

    A. great and honest representative
    B. wiser voice of the people than any statesman
    C. great beast
    D. undemocratic fool
    E. biased dullard

32. The union of two or more states into a larger state has, in history, been accomplished   32.____
    much more often through _____ than through _____.

    A. agreement; conquest
    B. indifference; military intervention
    C. hostilities with foreign powers; civil wars
    D. conquest; agreement
    E. peaceful legislation; blitzkrieg

33. The growth of states in size, by conquest and assimilation, has been shown to be   33.____

    A. nearly impossible in the twentieth century
    B. an orderly process
    C. an unlikely circumstance
    D. an irregular process
    E. invariably a product of military aggression

34. A military defense program in a modern nation is USUALLY initiated   34.____

    A. in times of great peril
    B. against a particular enemy
    C. at all times, in peace and war, by the people
    D. by the legislature
    E. in the hope of maintaining peace

35. Our urban industrial economy is highly competitive MAINLY because of   35.____

    A. the presence of minority groups
    B. man's antipathy to cooperation
    C. the desirability of the rewards
    D. the threat of Communism
    E. the growth of the suburbs

36. To widen the gap between what people want and what they actually have, the goal to be   36.____
    achieved would be widespread

    A. competition   B. discontent   C. cooperation
    D. self-destruction E. unemployment

37. The proportion of the American population living in villages has _____ in the last half   37.____
    century.

    A. increased
    B. decreased
    C. not changed much
    D. disappeared
    E. risen concomitantly with the urban population

38. When the American school system is examined, it is seen at once to reflect the _____ of the culture as a whole.

   A. decadence
   B. aspirations
   C. cooperative spirit
   D. competitive spirit
   E. simplicity

39. The group is always interested in transmitting its ideals to _____, for only in this way can the groups standards be preserved.

   A. the government
   B. the young
   C. industry
   D. other groups
   E. conquered neighbors

40. Birth control and planned families are increasing

   A. among the primitive tribes of New Guinea
   B. among Catholic countries
   C. among rural and wage-earning groups
   D. among the clergy
   E. because of a serious food shortage in the Western Hemisphere

41. The LEAST hazardous time of life, with reference to mortality, is

   A. infancy
   B. late childhood
   C. early middle age
   D. the prenatal stage
   E. old age

42. Total freedom is usually restricted by informal social pressures based upon _____, as well as by threats of retribution.

   A. religious doctrines
   B. the opinions of others
   C. government censorship
   D. statutes
   E. sound political theory

43. The movement of the American population is away from the

   A. more populous states
   B. East
   C. West
   D. agricultural areas
   E. suburbs

44. Malthus stated that, generally, a small population produces

   A. more children per family than a large population
   B. a lower standard of living
   C. a rapid rise in the birth rate
   D. a higher standard of living
   E. a decline in the birth rate

45. The population of an area may suffer loss in two ways, namely, _____ and _____.

   A. decline in birth rate; change of government
   B. migration; lowering of living standards
   C. decrease in wages; loss of industry
   D. death; emigration
   E. capitalism; war

46. Wars are not biologically inevitable.
There are several peoples who have never been known to have had a war; among these are the

    A. Bantus of Africa
    B. Sioux Indians
    C. Eskimos of Alaska
    D. Watusis of Africa
    E. Riffs of Morocco

47. The majority of marriages, past and present, throughout the entire world are

    A. polygamous
    B. monogamous
    C. polyandrous
    D. misogamous
    E. morganatic

48. In the Cooley tradition, a sociologist would learn to be _____ to the beautiful, complex ugliness of things as they are.

    A. indifferent
    B. alien
    C. generous
    D. hostile
    E. dispassionate

49. According to Cooley, the real interest of the American voter at election time is in

    A. economic issues
    B. party differences and compromises
    C. democratic principles
    D. the personalities of the candidates
    E. the sentiments expressed by the extreme right or the extreme left

50. Inherited characters are governed by an interplay of dominant and recessive genes. Of the following features of the human face, the ONLY dominant feature is

    A. concave nose
    B. thin lips
    C. red hair
    D. light eye color
    E. full lips

KEY (CORRECT ANSWERS)

1. E	11. A	21. E	31. C	41. B
2. B	12. C	22. B	32. D	42. B
3. D	13. B	23. B	33. D	43. D
4. D	14. A	24. E	34. B	44. D
5. D	15. D	25. C	35. C	45. D
6. A	16. E	26. A	36. B	46. C
7. A	17. A	27. C	37. C	47. B
8. C	18. B	28. C	38. D	48. C
9. A	19. D	29. E	39. B	49. D
10. A	20. C	30. C	40. B	50. E

EXAMINATION SECTION
TEST 1

DIRECTIONS: Each question or incomplete statement is followed by several suggested answers or completions. Select the one that BEST answers the question or completes the statement. *PRINT THE LETTER OF THE CORRECT ANSWER IN THE SPACE AT THE RIGHT.*

1. The crude death rate is derived by dividing a society's yearly deaths by its mid-year population AND

    A. dividing by 1000
    B. subtracting a fixed percentage to make up for inaccurate and unreliable reporting
    C. multiplying by 1,000
    D. multiplying by 500 to include embryonic mortality
    E. dividing by 100 to account for immigration and emigration

1.____

2. Western and Central Europe are considered to be

    A. lagging behind in cultural advancement
    B. secondary allies
    C. areas of stationary population
    D. industrially stagnant
    E. largely disaster areas

2.____

3. The units for the study of population are people. The classes of factors which influence these units are

    A. biological and geological
    B. mechanization, ability, and race
    C. men, money, and materials
    D. biological, social, and geographic
    E. sexual drives and instinctual protection of children

3.____

4. The statistical study of population is called

    A. popistatics   B. human ecology
    C. demography   D. statistography
    E. popography

4.____

5. Death rates are referred to as mortality rates. The morbidity rate

    A. is a secondary term for death rate
    B. signifies the incidence of disease
    C. refers to the number and percent of the population engaged in viewing monster pictures, gruesome spectacles, etc.
    D. is concerned with the number and percent of accidents
    E. pertains to death by violence

5.____

6. In Africa, there are many secret societies of ill fame, such as the *Leopards*. Such secret societies exist in many primitive cultures. In the United States, the _____ is an example of this type of society.

6.____

A. John Birch Society   B. Salvation Army
C. Ku Klux Klan   D. Shriners
E. Y.M.C.A.

7. A remarkable civilization developed from a simple, classless society prior to A.D. 1300 into a highly organized state in the fourteenth century. We are speaking of the _____ civilization.

    A. Eskimo   B. Aztec   C. Akamba
    D. Ashantis   E. Intichiuma

8. There are three great divisions in India's caste system. One of these is the _____, who were the agriculturalists and merchants.

    A. Kshatriyas   B. Brahmans   C. Vaisyas
    D. Sudanists   E. Gurus

9. Among primitives, breaches of the laws of exogamy are

    A. frequent and ignored
    B. always punishable by death
    C. the most serious in their whole moral code
    D. not regarded as serious by the *elders* or leaders of the tribe but will result in complete ostracism of the violator by the younger members of the group
    E. punishable by death or banishment from the tribe forever

10. Darwin showed that form

    A. follows beauty
    B. arises from disequilibrium
    C. is the modification of organisms
    D. must follow function
    E. supplants old conditions

11. Functional attitudes arise in experience and are crystallized out of it; they are

    A. primary, not secondary
    B. immutable and eternal
    C. simply there for us to find
    D. unchanging and ephemeral
    E. secondary, not primary

12. The Trobriand society is one in which

    A. the mother's brother assumes special responsibilities for his sister's child
    B. the women rule
    C. rank does not depend on one's clan or sub-clan
    D. the male members take over the care of the children and home while the female members hunt and assume governmental responsibilities
    E. the institution of the *Kula* (the sacrificing of animals to ceremonial gods) is of prime importance

13. _____ is fundamental to every form of human society.

    A. Virtue or evil
    B. Patriarchy or matriarchy
    C. Truth or dishonesty
    D. Reciprocity
    E. Reorientation

14. The _____ system is a very important determinant of social conduct in all primitive societies.

    A. capsian
    B. Minoan
    C. kinship
    D. dinaric
    E. numinous

15. Moral rules are not always considered absolute. Sociologists believe that they derive their value from

    A. their use by the upper classes in imposing their will on the lower classes
    B. their great diversity and flexibility
    C. transcendental principles independent of human experience
    D. their social utility
    E. the ability of the clergy to *sell* them in a package deal with God

16. In every society, _____ is prohibited, and the sanctity of contracts and bargains is enforced.

    A. exogamy
    B. killing
    C. usury
    D. dishonesty
    E. theft

17. All primitive societies maintain a strict system of etiquette controlling one's behavior towards other people. Among the rules of etiquette, none is so important as that governing _____ relationships.

    A. maternal
    B. impersonal
    C. joking
    D. potlatch
    E. business

18. Man needs faith and hope in order to continue the battle for subsistence. Primitive man was never without religion AND

    A. higher forms of art
    B. magic
    C. foresight
    D. artistic achievement
    E. musical ability

19. The primitive separates magic AND

    A. religion
    B. the forces which make good seasons and bad seasons
    C. the element of *luck* which he associates with agriculture
    D. strictly practical knowledge of his work or craft
    E. the religious rites performed to combat agricultural elements which he cannot understand

20. The various rain-making practices in which rain is *made* by sprinkling water or duplicating the process of precipitation would fall under the heading of _____ magic.

    A. contagious
    B. cumulative
    C. representative
    D. reproductive
    E. imitative

21. If the emphasis is on an impersonal source of power, or mana, which can be employed or trapped for human purposes, we call it *magic*. If it is on a semi-personal, non-material or spiritual being who may come to man's assistance, we call it

    A. numinous
    B. Christ
    C. animism
    D. magico-religious
    E. polytheism

22. The two contemporary theories which reject the evolution of culture are the diffusionist theory AND the

    A. culture-pattern theory
    B. convergence theory
    C. theory of running similarities
    D. independence theory
    E. theory of accidental discovery

23. Primitive societies are PARTICULARLY useful as a subject for study because

    A. it has been discovered that certain agricultural techniques of the primitives are far superior to our own
    B. it is the only yardstick by which civilized man can measure his cultural advancement
    C. they exhibit all the characteristics of a large society in a simplified form
    D. much can be learned from their systems of in-breeding
    E. they are constantly discovering new types of drugs in plant form

24. The _____ include the single existing genus, Homo, and all the fossil forms of man.

    A. anthropoids B. hominoids C. hylobates
    D. hominids   E. pongidae

25. The hand-ax industries, the flake industries, and the blade industries were three cultural elements of primary importance in the

    A. Iron Age   B. Pre-Glacial Period
    C. Copper Age   D. Old Stone Age
    E. Natufian Age

26. The first evidence of agriculture is found among the _____, who lived in the caves of Mount Carmel in Palestine.

    A. Hebrews   B. Mouflons
    C. Natufians   D. Pithecanthropus
    E. Bos Primigenius

27. Today we tend to divide man into three major races and several minor ones. These are

    A. so far as science is concerned, the original races of man
    B. not products of continuous evolution
    C. the final and ultimate races
    D. not the original races of man nor the final and ultimate race
    E. Caucasoid, Negroid, Mongoloid, Jews, Christians, and heathens

28. In primitive societies, pre-marital relations among the younger, unmarried persons is

   A. strictly forbidden
   B. sanctioned as long as the promise of marriage is witnessed by an elder or leader of the tribe
   C. sanctioned and, in some cases, is general, though regulated
   D. punishable by missionaries
   E. affirmatively demanded

29. In primitive societies, the transition from boyhood to manhood is

   A. regarded as normal and does not carry with it any added responsibilities
   B. usually marked by a *Bar Mitzvah* or confirmation ceremony
   C. marked by elaborate rites of initiation
   D. marked by a simple ceremony attended only by those of the immediate family
   E. simple compared to that of the French and Spanish peoples

30. The hominoids include

   A. Miocene apes and reptiles
   B. metazoa and protozoa
   C. anthropoid apes and man
   D. amphibians and man
   E. invertebrates and metazoa

31. Social classes appear only when the simple food-gathering economy

   A. collapses and is taken over by capitalism
   B. becomes profitable
   C. has given way to one involving agriculture, which provides a substantial surplus
   D. ceases to satisfy the leaders of the tribes
   E. is succeeded by a profit-sharing collaboration system

32. The Trobrianders are famous for their remarkable

   A. finger paintings
   B. prowess in hunting
   C. organization of a free society amidst chaos
   D. trading system
   E. contribution to art in the form of a brass-carving industry

33. When Mediterranean culture was flourishing under the Greeks and Romans,

   A. slaves obtained from Britain were considered the most valuable of any available
   B. Gaul and Britain were living in savagery
   C. Europeans began showing greater cultural achievements than the Mayan Indians
   D. a transformation was under way in Gaul and Britain
   E. the civilizations of Egypt and Mesopotamia were developing in isolation

34. The original meaning of pastoralism was

   A. the purification of milk
   B. the herding of cattle
   C. an association of ministers
   D. challenged by Louis Pasteur
   E. the cultivation of plants

35. In a primitive society, one cannot marry whom one likes. one can, however, seek marriage with a

    A. parallel cousin
    B. member of one's own group
    C. cousin within the family, if several degrees distant
    D. cross cousin
    E. cousin of the same age

36. Down through the ages, war has helped bring about an interesting and major discovery; namely, that man

    A. has always been bent on total destruction
    B. hates war
    C. as well as animals can be domesticated
    D. in spite of civilization, still lives by the savage laws of the jungle because he has an inherent love of violence
    E. can never fully appreciate peace unless he has fought and killed for it

37. The Alpine, Nordic, and Mediterranean are

    A. the easiest groups to identify
    B. found in Southern France and south of the Sahara
    C. people whose skin color ranges from *light* to dark-brown or *black*
    D. three subdivisions of the Caucasoid race
    E. those who are born in the mountains and by the sea

38. The Pleistocene was the period of the Ice Age in Europe. It was the last period of the Cenozoic era AND was

    A. marked by continuous cold
    B. the dawn of life itself
    C. highlighted by the emergence of the invertebrates
    D. an era of renascense since it gave birth to the most advanced forms of agricultural development
    E. the period in which man evolved

39. Between the Old Stone Age and the New Stone Age,

    A. the use of the tool was discovered
    B. came the Mesolithic period
    C. agriculture was invented
    D. man began to hunt
    E. man discovered fire

40. _____ was used in Mesopotamia and Egypt in 2500 B.C.

    A. Bronze   B. Iron   C. Copper
    D. Aluminum   E. Steel

41. The Man from LaChapelle was

    A. discovered by Dawson in 1912 in a cave near Bonn
    B. the title under which the French revolutionist, Jean Le Bais, carried on his fight for the Free French Society in 1728
    C. the title given to a German World War I song by the French
    D. a cave man who used Mousterian flint tools
    E. the more human type of man who immediately preceded Heidelberg man

42. Rhodesian man has been described as an extremely rugged form of

    A. the ape-like creatures from the Miocene period
    B. Cretaceous man
    C. Neanderthal man, evidencing racial senility and bony excrescences
    D. the man-ape species found in Choukoutien
    E. Java man, and exhibiting an extremely small cranial area

43. Up until a few years ago, many people wanted to believe that we had descended ONLY from the _____ (possibly because they seemed to be the best looking).

    A. Neanderthals   B. Perthes   C. Cro-Magnons
    D. Yahgans   E. Piltdowns

44. Anthropologists point out that the *human type* has survived MAINLY because

    A. of its ability to adapt to its environment
    B. he realizes that it is only the strong who survive
    C. of its tools and superior housing conditions
    D. he has learned how to execute his enemies and exploit his friends
    E. of its cooperative nature

45. With the last phase of the Old Stone Age, we entered a new world peopled by

    A. Shamans and expert tool users
    B. our own species, with complex and imaginative ideas
    C. Dryopithecus, who may have been the first men to invade Southern Europe
    D. Cro-Magnons, of great intelligence, who contributed to history by writing the Cephalic Index
    E. Dinarics, a racial group originating in Yugoslavia

46. Anthropologists are aware of a certain _____ in primitive societies, insofar as they have avoided too close contact with technologically advanced civilizations.

    A. inconsistency   B. precocity   C. stability
    D. volition   E. stagnation

47. One of the ways in which American society differs from primitive society is

    A. in the efforts of Americans to attain status
    B. in its religious tendencies
    C. that the former is generally more intelligent
    D. in the emergence of an owning and managing class
    E. in its superior understanding of its fellow man

48. Capsian is

    A. a genus of fossil hominoid found in South Africa
    B. a central Australian ceremony, the purpose of which is to supply food through certain magical activities assigned to the totem groups
    C. the doctrine that objects and persons may be possessed by spirits that are not their own souls
    D. a method of writing characterized by wedge-shaped signs impressed on clay tablets
    E. a late-paleolithic blade culture in North Africa

49. The practice of requiring or permitting a man to marry the widow of his brother is called

    A. gynocracy   B. dinaricism
    C. levirate   D. dolichocephalicism
    E. albinism

50. The Marching Rule refers to

    A. a system of exchanging goods in New Guinea
    B. certain groups within a tribe with secret membership and activities which are usually devoted to the drawing up of religious documents
    C. a Central Australian custom by which the leader of a tribe is required to march many miles without food or water to prove his strength and right to continue as ruler
    D. a postwar native movement in the Pacific Islands and Admiralty Islands, whereby strict codes of behavior were drawn up and villages were rebuilt on modern lines
    E. a document of *peace* drawn up between the Malayans and the Europeans

KEY (CORRECT ANSWERS)

1. C	11. E	21. C	31. C	41. D
2. C	12. A	22. A	32. D	42. C
3. D	13. D	23. C	33. B	43. C
4. C	14. C	24. D	34. B	44. E
5. B	15. D	25. D	35. D	45. B
6. C	16. E	26. C	36. C	46. C
7. B	17. C	27. D	37. D	47. D
8. C	18. B	28. C	38. E	48. E
9. C	19. D	29. C	39. B	49. C
10. D	20. E	30. C	40. B	50. D

TEST 2

DIRECTIONS: Each question or incomplete statement is followed by several suggested answers or completions. Select the one that BEST answers the question or completes the statement. *PRINT THE LETTER OF THE CORRECT ANSWER IN THE SPACE AT THE RIGHT.*

1. In some areas of the world, racial interbreeding is common and usually carries no social stigma. In India and America,

    A. such interbreeding is gradually becoming the accepted social pattern
    B. the half-caste passes unnoticed
    C. the offspring of mixed marriages are not accepted as being responsible members of society
    D. the half-caste may suffer social ostracism
    E. the half-caste will find refuge from the social stigmas imposed upon him by the more tradition-minded European societies

    1._____

2. American society has taken steps to reverse disorganizing trends in the family. One of these steps has led to the

    A. strict supervision of the content of family magazines
    B. setting up of a fund devoted to the care and counseling of those involved with social work
    C. organization of The Council on Human Relations in Society
    D. establishment of The National Council on Family Affairs
    E. founding of an organization known as The Fun Family, which has introduced an exciting and novel approach to family amusement

    2._____

3. In human ecology, six principal processes are at work in communites: concentration, centralization, decentralization, segregation, succession, and

    A. obversion   B. invasion   C. desegregation
    D. inversion   E. integration

    3._____

4. Freud has shown that the suppression of the pleasure principle by the reality principle was

    A. wanton and unnecessary
    B. necessary in order to thwart materialistic social institutions
    C. required in order that civilization might develop
    D. brought about by guilt at wanting pleasure and feeling unworthy of it
    E. the first step toward cultural and artistic development

    4._____

5. Art exists in primitive society for

    A. psychological and social reasons
    B. the advancement of religious tendencies
    C. the same reason it exists anywhere else
    D. reasons that civilized man may never quite comprehend
    E. itself, and needs no reasons or excuses for its existence

    5._____

6. In talking of marriage, most people profess to believe in the dictates of love and the principles of equality, but

   A. inevitably the *dream* of an ocean of devotion gives way to the *demand* for *a puddle of prosperity*
   B. man wants nothing to do with double standards
   C. nine out of ten marriages take place as they would in the strictest of caste systems
   D. necessity makes love and equality a bitter pill to swallow
   E. they discover, all too soon, the impracticality of such beliefs

7. Which one of the following factors is NOT responsible for racial differentiation?

   A. Natural selection
   B. Gene mutation
   C. Population mixtures
   D. Class selection
   E. Genetic drift

8. It is generally realized today that intelligence testing often yields unreliable results. This may be caused by the

   A. atmosphere surrounding this type of testing, that it is not conducive to obtaining preferred results
   B. difficulty in separating innate or *pure* intelligence from the effects of social training
   C. great resentment most people feel toward anything which appears to question or test their intellectual capacity
   D. reality that primitive man cannot be expected to possess so much intellect as civilized man
   E. fact that overlapping makes the task of testing different races too complicated

9. From the condition of bones found in the Peking Man's stomping grounds, we can PROPERLY assume that

   A. he had the ability to utilize fire and make tools
   B. he suffered from certain bone diseases of the legs
   C. he was a cannibal
   D. his back was curved and bent because he carried most of his possessions, at all times, with him
   E. he made his first appearance prior to the Ice Age

10. The Indians of Tierra del Fuego will be extinct within a few years. Nearly all of them have been destroyed by

    A. their complete lack of social organization
    B. their exhaustion of natural resources
    C. the diseases and ways of the white man
    D. their inability to improve their methods of food gathering
    E. their low level of literacy

11. Americans, as a group, tend to disregard

    A. racial differences
    B. culture
    C. ancestors' social status
    D. poverty
    E. a high or low level of economic development

12. An *institution* is

    A. a formal organization
    B. the basic unit of society
    C. devoted to cultural advancement
    D. not an organization
    E. a place where disturbed people can find recreation

13. Placing a child in the Boy Scouts is an example of

    A. forced conformity
    B. static adaptation
    C. deliberate socialization
    D. status-seeking on the part of the parents
    E. patriarchal dominance

14. Both the *crowd* and the *mob* function

    A. with the aid of social approval
    B. without discussion and reflection
    C. in a highly sophisticated manner
    D. within social boundaries
    E. in conformance with the *rule of reason*

15. Complex societies are _____ societies which reveal broad variations in culture.

    A. anomic   B. inferior   C. heterogeneous
    D. sanctional E. heteromorphous

16. Socialization is deliberate but

    A. rational   B. concentrated   C. specialized
    D. neurotic   E. unconscious

17. Sociology is most like political science in that

    A. it deals with physical needs
    B. its academicians are usually communists or fascists
    C. it deals with the social world
    D. it is a product of rationales and fantasies
    E. its theories are invariably borne out by events

18. For a political organization to be truly stable, it must

    A. distribute its power equally among competing groups
    B. abolish voluntary and eleemosynary associations
    C. remove independent groups from society
    D. anticipate world needs
    E. abolish war and capital punishment

19. One of the goals which Castro and Yeltsin purport to have in common is the

    A. eventual humiliation of the common man
    B. right of the common man to select his own leaders
    C. eventual achievement of *practical* anarchy

D. burning of the *Blue Book*
E. eventual emancipation and elevation of the common man

20. Social group work is one method in the profession of social work. One other method is 20.____

    A. socialized religion
    B. socialized medical work
    C. union establishment
    D. social case work
    E. organized labor

21. Social group work ALWAYS implies 21.____

    A. the giving of certain sums of money to impoverished families
    B. a worker from outside the group
    C. interference with the lives of other people
    D. changes in the basic culture of people
    E. an indifference toward the individual

22. *Character building, leisure time, recreational and informal education* are 22.____

    A. some of the factors psychologists are studying in relation to society
    B. not accepted by most agencies as having much to do with social betterment
    C. some of the names which have been applied to agencies in which group work is carried on
    D. factors which organized religion is trying to do away with
    E. words which have no real meaning to the poverty-stricken

23. In the beginning, the social worker should place prime emphasis on 23.____

    A. securing complete cooperation from the group
    B. group organization
    C. planning
    D. the importance of the group's understanding of the problems involved in social work
    E. warmth and friendliness

24. Perhaps the greatest single element in the beginning stages of work with a group is the 24.____

    A. attainment of respect and almost *blind faith* on the part of the group
    B. worker's ability to accept the group *as it is*
    C. possession of a broad sense of humor
    D. ability to bring together members with similar problems and personality traits
    E. ability to raise enough money to support the group properly

25. In working with a group, it is necessary for the social worker to 25.____

    A. have private meetings with each individual at least once every week
    B. allow members to express negative feelings
    C. keep constant order and rule the group with force, if necessary
    D. stress positive feelings in the members and avoid, if at all possible, any show of negative behavior on the part of the members
    E. keep the topics of conversation and discussion interesting and exciting

26. Agencies must fashion a sound policy on grouping by analyzing these four basic factors: agency purpose, community situation, agency resources, and 26.____

    A. available personnel
    B. available funds
    C. general knowledge of groups and their influence on individuals
    D. degree of racial integration
    E. general knowledge of what each religious group will permit

27. The ONLY way in which a group worker can determine the stage of development of the group is to 27.____

    A. study the behavior of each individual member of the group
    B. study the behavior responses of the group individually and collectively
    C. discontinue the *pre-group* stages temporarily and study the reaction
    D. ask each member individually what his feelings are on the subject
    E. consult the records of the group

28. All groups at one time or another feel hostile toward their worker or agency, and such behavior is 28.____

    A. dangerous and must be suppressed at once
    B. best alleviated by ejecting the hostile protagonists from the group
    C. normal and should be handled as such
    D. usually a sign that the agency or worker is lacking in some way
    E. not helpful to the group or worker and, therefore, the best solution is to terminate the meetings until such feelings have subsided

29. To a group worker, the writing of records and reports is 29.____

    A. not necessary but can be a useful aid to his job
    B. an important part of his responsibility
    C. unimportant compared to the more *human* aspects of his job
    D. an uninteresting and unexciting part of his job that must be done
    E. clinical and impersonal, and has no place in the area of true social work

30. Newly developed areas have special needs for community-subsidized leisure-time services designed to 30.____

    A. develop a *sense of neighborhood*
    B. bring the children together in a safe and healthy environment
    C. develop a *sense of concentration* in the community
    D. bring about *community pride*
    E. develop a feeling of independence

31. A labor dispute between employer and employees which ends in a strike is basically 31.____

    A. unconstitutional, according to some sociologists
    B. a conflict situation
    C. an example of antipathetical relationships involving power tactics
    D. regretted by both sides
    E. and, frequently, a spiritual and cleansing experience

32. Culture, or social heritage, surrounds social relationships in at least two ways. It provides a set of values and

   A. seeks to utilize mythological beliefs in justification of existence
   B. a set of norms
   C. sociofacts
   D. a sound platform on which modern man can stand
   E. attempts to show the way to idealized thinking

33. China's antiquity can be used to point out that

   A. poverty can win out
   B. deep religious beliefs enable even the most impoverished to survive
   C. a peasant society can survive for thousands of years
   D. contrary to most beliefs, the old ways are the safest and the best
   E. the old way is not always the best way

34. Symbolically, which of the following patterns would a conformist society attempt to alter?

35. *Belonging* is related to

   A. voluntary help
   B. program and platform
   C. people and purpose
   D. an intellectual experience
   E. organization and disintegration

36. Comte is sometimes referred to as the

   A. *Father of Free Thinking*
   B. *Founder of Social Work*
   C. *Father of Religion*
   D. *Father of Sociology*
   E. *Father of Free Love*

37. Vast social changes have occurred that have NOT been connected in any way with

   A. cultural revisions made in the last fifty years
   B. changes in racial type
   C. the desires of the common man in society
   D. the Industrial Revolution
   E. the good of the people

38. Among the great apes, only the gorilla joined man in

   A. using implements to aid his daily life
   B. the use of *bluffing* to ward off enemies
   C. taking up a life primarily oriented to the ground
   D. irreverant mimicry of characteristic frailties
   E. taking part in perverted or exploiting practices

39. The word *geneticist* is derived from the Greek word for

    A. follower of ancient cultures
    B. talker about ancient beings
    C. walker about the earth
    D. birth follower
    E. singer of man's virtues

40. It was in the Middle East, in the *Fertile Crescent,* that

    A. the first sign of man's belief in a world beyond was discovered
    B. human civilization began ten thousand years ago
    C. the first traces of the Piltdown man were found
    D. mongoloid religion was believed to have begun
    E. human civilization began more than 20,000 years ago

41. *World, we don't suit each other, you and I, and you're going to change* may have been said or thought by early man when he first

    A. got religion
    B. understood that the world was not there solely for his existence
    C. felt the presence of God
    D. decided to move to more appropriate living quarters
    E. changed the shape of a stone

42. The Heidelberg jawbone was

    A. found beside the skull of a Peking woman, thereby disproving many scientific theories
    B. a seventeenth century discovery
    C. the biggest hoax perpetrated on science since the Piltdown episode
    D. Europe's oldest trace of man
    E. the earliest trace of man in America

43. The Eskimos, South African Bushmen, Shoshones, and African Pigmies are some of the groups using the simple food-gathering systems. In order to survive, these groups must

    A. place more emphasis on formal education, especially on the part of the male members of their groups
    B. be absorbed into higher forms of civilization
    C. improve working conditions to allow more free time in which to advance the cultural aspects of their society
    D. appoint leaders of all food-gathering groups in order to assure a continuous food supply
    E. seek an effective means of protection for themselves and their cultures against the invasion of so-called reformers

44. It CANNOT be claimed that the pigmy hunter of the Congo forests, in comparison with the European or American factory worker,

    A. can adjust to change of any kind
    B. cannot continue to live without revisions of some kind in his way of life
    C. lives a life less well-adjusted
    D. lives a less profitable community life
    E. lives a less satisfactory life

45. The white man can be proud of his inventions and discoveries. It is questionable, however,

    A. whether or not humanity really needs them
    B. whether these achievements have brought greater happiness, as yet, to mankind as a whole
    C. how much longer and further he can advance if attitudes remain as they are
    D. whether the rest of the world will follow suit
    E. whether or not these have been overrated

46. Whenever we are inclined to describe a human culture as stagnant or stationary, we must

    A. understand that all cultures are not so fortunate as our own
    B. accept the fact that lack of religion is usually responsible for this condition
    C. ponder the fact that some cultures are inferior to others
    D. ask ourselves whether its apparent immobility may not result from our ignorance of its true interests
    E. realize that poverty is probably the cause

47. Evidence provided by tests of mental ability appears to give strong support to the hypothesis that

    A. all men have basic mental qualities of the same kind
    B. no one can apply himself to that which is unfamiliar
    C. all men have the ability to learn similar things
    D. certain religious or ethnic groups learn more quickly than others
    E. all men are created equal insofar as the capacity to learn new things is equal

48. Which of the following is considered to be a status symbol? The

    A. size of a company's letterhead
    B. location of a desk in an office
    C. color of a new automobile
    D. number of paintings in an office
    E. quality of the paintings in a home

49. Prison riots are NOT usually staged

    A. to gain recognition
    B. to express dissatisfaction
    C. in order to escape
    D. to improve the quality of the food served
    E. to attract the attention of some committee

50. Authoritarianism is another name for

    A. republicanism   B. democracy   C. monarchy
    D. dictatorship   E. socialism

KEY (CORRECT ANSWERS)

1. D	11. C	21. B	31. B	41. E
2. D	12. D	22. C	32. B	42. D
3. B	13. C	23. E	33. C	43. B
4. C	14. B	24. B	34. E	44. C
5. A	15. C	25. B	35. C	45. B
6. C	16. E	26. C	36. D	46. D
7. D	17. C	27. B	37. B	47. A
8. B	18. A	28. C	38. C	48. B
9. C	19. E	29. B	39. D	49. C
10. C	20. D	30. A	40. B	50. D

EXAMINATION SECTION
TEST 1

DIRECTIONS: Each question or incomplete statement is followed by several suggested answers or completions. Select the one that BEST answers the question or completes the statement. *PRINT THE LETTER OF THE CORRECT ANSWER IN THE SPACE AT THE RIGHT.*

1. The *principle of limited possibilities* is the belief

    A. in the law of averages
    B. in certain basic, worldwide culture forms
    C. that the ability of the Black to rise above his station is contained
    D. in inevitable unemployment within minority groups
    E. that certain primitive cultures are limited in their range of advancement

    1._____

2. The suburban dweller is expected to develop

    A. much less originality than his city brother
    B. a greater sense of family security than the city dweller
    C. a greater sense of identification with his community than the city dweller
    D. a greater sense of accomplishment in regard to small things than the city dweller
    E. a greater respect for nature than a person who comes from the city

    2._____

3. In systematic crime,

    A. it is found that more than 40% of the criminals are thirty-five or over
    B. training and skill are necessary for advancement
    C. there is no loyalty among the members of a crime syndicate
    D. it is impossible to distinguish brain from brawn
    E. there is little opportunity for advancement

    3._____

4. *Dago, Guinea,* and *Kraut* are

    A. words which refer distastefully to certain areas of different countries
    B. words which reflect animosity toward different cultures
    C. some types of organizations which are discriminated against
    D. descriptions which symbolize hostilities against nationality groups
    E. exotic continental labels

    4._____

5. The sociological approach to understanding war recognizes it as

    A. a complex phenomenon with multiple causes
    B. part of the natural law of the survival of the fittest
    C. basic to human nature
    D. possessing a positive value
    E. the inevitable outcome of capitalist competition among nations

    5._____

6. The suicide rate is HIGHEST among the

    A. divorced   B. married   C. unmarried
    D. widowed   E. separated

    6._____

7. _____ is the name given to a technique which involves an interesting combination of pure and applied science.

   A. Direct observation
   B. Field study
   C. Case study
   D. Action research
   E. Participant-observer

8. The median score is

   A. derived from a concept developed by Freud
   B. an equal number of items away from each of the extremes
   C. a line which is drawn between different social classes
   D. a partial and incomplete division
   E. a piece of music written in the 17th century by a member of the Median tribe

9. Plato is important in the history of sociology because he

   A. developed an important theory of suicide
   B. was essentially a philosopher
   C. developed certain speculative philosophical theories about man and society
   D. was the first to connect man's inability to function philosophically with the social impositions made upon him
   E. essayed the first practical steps toward the study of sociological problems

10. A marked tendency to identify minorities in ways that accentuate differences is exhibited by

    A. prison authorities in general
    B. those whose literary level is subnormal
    C. groups with minimum educational opportunities
    D. the less unlightened sociologists
    E. Americans

11. Those sociologists who endorse capital punishment on what they consider objective grounds USUALLY center their arguments on which one of the following concepts?

    A. An eye for an eye, a tooth for a tooth
    B. Capital punishment is a deterrent to potential offenders
    C. Killing produces a need for righteousness and excitement
    D. The population of our prisons needs to be thinned out
    E. A criminal who has committed an enormously evil crime can never be rehabilitated

12. If a saleswoman says, *You should purchase this dress because they're all wearing them*, this would be an example of

    A. poor salesmanship
    B. the assumption that no one wants to be different, and conformity is an assurance of success
    C. fear of disruption and change of any kind in daily living
    D. conflicting norms
    E. ignorance of fashion trends

13. Human beings possess a biological sex drive which is a necessary condition for procreation.
    The maternal care and paternal protection of children

    A. is a natural instinct
    B. contrary to many beliefs, is not instinctual
    C. is brought about, to a large extent, by the fear of retaliation
    D. is due largely to a strange kind of pity toward the weak and innocent
    E. stems from the egotistical desire to protect what is *theirs*

    13.____

14. Group isolations result in

    A. a greater degree of individuality
    B. anti-social moves of a dangerous nature
    C. the weakening of social control
    D. the founding, in most cases, of varied and original types of culture
    E. irresponsible and politically unhealthy attitudes toward society as a whole

    14.____

15. A change in customs leads to

    A. a change in mores
    B. a loosening of racial boundaries
    C. a decline of civilization in the broadest sense
    D. probable extinction of a sect or group
    E. the beginning of a *growing up* process

    15.____

16. Charles Horton Cooley introduced the concept of

    A. preliminary observation   B. the primary group
    C. field study work   D. pre-group activation
    E. free mind initiation

    16.____

17. All groups NOT in accord with the definition of a primary group are classified as

    A. pre-groups   B. race-originated
    C. caste groups or systems   D. face-to-face groups
    E. secondary groups

    17.____

18. When restrictions of caste do not prevail and a person is able to move into a different class,

    A. the result in anarchy
    B. the class system is said to be *open*
    C. he does so at the risk of having nothing to fall back on if his new-found *home* does not suit him
    D. he must usually renounce all previous commitments, whether religious or political
    E. the result is the debasement of the society

    18.____

19. Sociologists have developed three techniques for determining class lines. They are the subjective approach, the objective approach, and the _____ approach.

    A. historical   B. observant   C. reputational
    D. categorical   E. intuitive

    19.____

20. Some sociologists use the word *assumption* where an individual

    A. takes on added responsibilities
    B. feels he is *just as good as the next guy*
    C. voluntarily changes his status by choosing parenthood or turning from one profession to another
    D. crashes the caste barrier and expects no repercussion
    E. obviously of low class, assumes the right to partake of food in the same dining area with his superiors

21. The *American Dream* concept is evident in one of the following sentences:

    A. Might makes Right
    B. Any little boy can grow up to be president
    C. We must rid America of the Edward Albees and all they stand for
    D. We can beat Russia any day
    E. Last one to the Moon's a dirty toad

22. His walls are panelled to keep out the cold winds. The soft hum of the air conditioner soothes him in the summer, and the muted tones of Muzak are all but absorbed by the heavy pile rug.
    HE is the

    A. owner of a supermarket
    B. junior clerk
    C. social investigator
    D. senior executive
    E. junior associate of a law firm

23. Membership in voluntary associations increases as

    A. family ties get stronger
    B. status increases and class goes up
    C. societies become more industrialized
    D. people grow older and their need for companionship increases
    E. people move to California or Monaco

24. Sociological research findings in the United States suggest that _____ is PROBABLY of more immediate consequence in moulding conduct among people than power or class.

    A. brotherhood   B. understanding   C. coercion
    D. money   E. status

25. The American system of public education, having developed vested interests, values, order, and stability, and having contributed to the integration of society is

    A. still sorely lacking in efficiency
    B. an organization
    C. not concerned with the problems of the individual
    D. an institution
    E. in need of more personnel with doctoral degrees

26. An association is an organized group.
An institution

    A. refers to the church and the family
    B. is a formal organization
    C. is an organized procedure
    D. deals with value infusions
    E. is the establishment of a social base

27. According to political scientists and sociologists, a public

    A. consists of people in one geographic area
    B. comes into being wherever and whenever an issue arises
    C. is a formal organization
    D. is structured, unlike a crowd or mob which is unstructured
    E. is generally emotion-dominated

28. Statistics show that suicides occur more often

    A. during peacetime
    B. because of loneliness among people with little or no intelligence
    C. during depressions and war
    D. among those who have never belonged to a church or religious order
    E. among disillusioned businessmen

29. Civic welfare is GREATER

    A. wherever the intelligence level is greater
    B. in the small city
    C. in the poorer areas of any city
    D. only through understanding the exact needs of a community
    E. in rural areas

30. Despite the increase in divorce,

    A. the married couple of today is better adjusted to life, generally, than the married couple of a decade ago
    B. there have been important changes made in divorce laws to make this procedure difficult and, in many cases, impossible in the United States
    C. more families stay together for the benefit of offspring than ever before
    D. there have been no important changes in the laws governing divorce in the United States
    E. less research is being conducted to determine its causes than in the past

31. A peasant society is USUALLY

    A. made up of highly individual types
    B. one with little or no restrictions placed upon the behavior patterns of its members
    C. highly complex
    D. village-centered
    E. without hope of change or status

32. The FIRST major pillar of peasant life is

    A. religion   B. the community   C. the family
    D. commerce   E. local government

33. The peculiarity of the crowd-mind lies MAINLY in

    A. its total lack of consideration or discussion of any kind
    B. in the ignorance it preys upon to launch or communicate its feelings
    C. in the readiness with which any communicable feeling is spread and augmented
    D. in the strength it feels in being in contact with emotions or ideas as a whole
    E. its invariable wrongheadedness

34. Like everything else that has power in human life, the money-strong represent the

    A. ideal of freedom
    B. stabilizing element of society as a whole
    C. the survival of the fittest, in some sense
    D. survival of the best
    E. highest intellectual elements of human life

35. The minds of the majority mould their ideals MOSTLY from

    A. the spectacle of visible and tangible success
    B. their respected ancestors
    C. familiar maxims
    D. formulas and polls
    E. cynicism and disillusionment

36. In a society where there is some freedom of opportunity, ambitious and intelligent men are an element of importance.
    The CHIEF aim of most of these men who come from a lower class of society seems to be to

    A. raise the standard of the lower class
    B. improve their status and position in the lower class
    C. get out of the lower class
    D. improve the lower class, thereby giving equal opportunity to all its members
    E. find a means that will enable them to adjust to their station

37. It is a COMMON opinion that the sway of riches over the human mind

    A. can only result in the total destruction of the world
    B. is greater in America and in our time than ever before
    C. stems from lack of education
    D. is enforced mainly by parental values
    E. leads many people of a high intellectual level into social work

38. Changing family characteristics in the United States include the

    A. slackening of interest in art
    B. decline of paternal authority
    C. inability to accept religion in its present form
    D. sapping of social fraternization
    E. loss of the mother image

39. One of the BASIC causes of family breakdown is   39._____

    A. sexual incompatibility
    B. the stark problem of delinquency
    C. the inability to face the ordeal of communication between partners
    D. the fear of financial destruction
    E. the fundamental incompatibility of roles

40. Sociologists hold that role playing   40._____

    A. is unhealthy and dangerous
    B. is, in effect, a childish attempt to overcome insecurity
    C. may be unconscious
    D. exists only in strained and unnatural atmospheres
    E. is a conscious striving for self-importance

41. The popular stereotypes of married life are regarded by social scientists as   41._____

    A. being very close to the actualities
    B. erroneous
    C. a strong clue to the realities of the situation
    D. containing more than a grain of truth
    E. being biologically, if not scientifically, sound

42. Social control deteriorates when families do not or cannot   42._____

    A. contribute to cultural aims
    B. alter their role in the prevention of juvenile crime
    C. submit themselves to compromising situations
    D. perform their rightful socializing role
    E. subscribe to religious doctrines of a conflicting nature

43. Those persons who are prejudiced are also, USUALLY,   43._____

    A. ignorant
    B. victims of parental indoctrination
    C. conforming to their own group norms
    D. victims of inferior education
    E. found in groups whose income level is low

44. In the culture of Brazil, it is found that social distinctions   44._____

    A. do not exist   B. are based on class
    C. are based on race   D. do not affect life or work
    E. are based on religion

45. Minority problems are   45._____

    A. found to exist mostly in the United States
    B. based entirely on cultural differences
    C. worldwide
    D. completely ignored in America
    E. becoming less important in the Western world

46. It is true that *job roles*

    A. is a concept that is most closely associated with European societies
    B. is a problem brought about mostly by insecurity
    C. exist only in the United States
    D. are an imaginary assumption
    E. alter personalities

47. One-half of American workers today

    A. are being paid minimum wages
    B. are in service industries
    C. are closer to poverty than at any other time in the history of the United States
    D. are in a higher income bracket than one-fourth of the supervisory and executive personnel
    E. belong to the middle and upper classes

48. The type of social organization which must be developed for totalitarianism to be successful is

    A. deistic   B. monolithic   C. capitalistic
    D. pluralistic   E. masochistic

49. The social *penalty* of a pluralistic system is

    A. the complete loss of individuality
    B. the temporary enslavement of the *life force*
    C. the surrendering of all previously held beliefs
    D. compromise
    E. twelve to fifteen years in a *prison* of doubt and discontent

50. In studies of the sociology of politics, it has been found that parties tend to identify with

    A. the most physically appealing candidate
    B. the aims of pressure groups
    C. anything which purports to be the *American Way*
    D. the man (candidate) who talks longest and loudest
    E. anything which upholds freedom and democracy

KEY (CORRECT ANSWERS)

1. B	11. B	21. B	31. D	41. B
2. C	12. B	22. D	32. C	42. D
3. B	13. B	23. B	33. C	43. C
4. D	14. C	24. E	34. C	44. B
5. A	15. A	25. D	35. A	45. C
6. A	16. B	26. C	36. C	46. E
7. D	17. E	27. B	37. B	47. B
8. B	18. B	28. A	38. B	48. B
9. C	19. C	29. B	39. E	49. D
10. E	20. C	30. D	40. C	50. B

TEST 2

DIRECTIONS: Each question or incomplete statement is followed by several suggested answers or completions. Select the one that BEST answers the question or completes the statement. *PRINT THE LETTER OF THE CORRECT ANSWER IN THE SPACE AT THE RIGHT.*

1. The assumption by primates of an arboreal existence led to

    A. the invertebrates
    B. the Oligocene Age
    C. improvements in sensory perception and the use of hands
    D. the development of claws and intensification of the sense of smell
    E. the eventual laying down of sedimentary rocks, leading in turn to the first evidences of life and habitation in the fossiliferous rock

1.____

2. The profile of a _____ skull shows a retreating forehead, heavy eyebrow ridges, and an elongated brain case, which varies in size from 1400 cc. to 1600 cc. The chin, though sloping, is less muzzlelike than that of more primitive forms of man.

    A. Simian   B. Australopithecus
    C. Pithecanthropus IV   D. Neanderthal
    E. Cro-Magnon

2.____

3. Inherited characteristics are governed by an interplay of dominant and recessive genes. Of the following features of the human face, the ONLY dominant feature is

    A. concave nose   B. thin lips
    C. red hair   D. light eye color
    E. full lips

3.____

4. Man stands firmly and can balance himself securely due to the remarkable development of the foot; in this regard, we term man

    A. Paleoanthropic   B. Plantigrade
    C. Numinous   D. Anthropoid
    E. Homo sapiens

4.____

5. A smaller brain, in a given race, such as the Pigmy, is indicative of

    A. their gradual extinction
    B. a lesser intelligence
    C. a smaller build
    D. the type of climate which is necessary for their survival
    E. their particular tribal concepts

5.____

6. While man's primary need is food, his SECONDARY need is

    A. shelter
    B. protection from his environment
    C. tools
    D. clothing
    E. culture

6.____

7. Margaret Mead has pointed out that an American man who wants to win recognition should be, FIRST,

   A. concerned with his relationship to his fellow man in society
   B. a success in his business
   C. cognizant of the ideals of democracy
   D. a head of a family unit
   E. psychologically healthy

8. Sociology is based on the belief that

   A. all human endeavor and progress is the result of individual thought
   B. human actions must be performed for the ultimate good of society
   C. all races and religions can live in harmony
   D. poverty and *class* systems will become non-existent
   E. the use of the scientific method is the key to new discoveries about man's collective character

9. Man is not *naturally* gregarious.
   He must be taught to form groups, and this teaching takes place BEGINNING with

   A. observation of other forms of animal life
   B. the concept of majority and minority groups
   C. the protective care of his family
   D. the school and social contacts made then
   E. his earliest choices of companions

10. Norms are effective as long as the rewards of _____ are worth it.

    A. work   B. conformity   C. ambition
    D. survival   E. iconoclasm

11. Whenever competition is conscious and deliberate, _____ develops.

    A. free enterprise   B. a better product
    C. choice   D. organization
    E. rivalry

12. _____ represent norms that appear in societies with some form of political organization and are enacted by society.

    A. Folkways   B. Rules   C. Mores
    D. Laws   E. Customs

13. An extended family is termed *bilateral,* which means it includes

    A. husband, wife, and children
    B. relatives of both husband and wife
    C. all children of a polygamous marriage
    D. the patrilineal family
    E. polygamy

14. MOST people are monogamously married because

    A. the religions of the world favor monogamy
    B. the family-unit concept demands it

C. it is obviously the fairest and most equitable system
D. society profits from it
E. the sexes are roughly equal in number

15. Wife-sharing has been practiced (and explained as a necessary pledge that a guest is a friend and not an enemy) by the

   A. Africans B. Eskimos C. Javanese
   D. Samoans E. Tahitians

16. In a primitive society, one cannot marry whom one likes or anyone in one's own group; hence the term

   A. polyandry B. exogamy C. gynocracy
   D. matrilocal E. patrilocal

17. Incestuous unions are the source of very powerful taboos; their origin and reason is

   A. a high rate of mortality
   B. biological
   C. that negative or recessive genes are often involved
   D. social
   E. based upon religious beliefs

18. The study of population, sometimes called _____, is concerned with the number of people to be found in a certain area, often cross-referred to according to age and sex.

   A. demography B. ecology C. numerology
   D. statistics E. ethnology

19. There are three kinds of change which can overtake a primitive community. The FIRST may be exemplified by a native adopting a steel tool instead of a stone implement and is termed

   A. divine B. voluntary C. practical
   D. adaptation E. hysteresis

20. A society of much interest to anthropologists, where wars do not exist, a child may have many mothers, and which encourages adolescent sexual experimentation, is found in

   A. Samoa B. Tibet
   C. the Trobriand Islands D. Galapagos
   E. New Guinea

21. The term sociology, meaning the social relationships of man and society as evaluated by scientific methods, was coined by the philosopher

   A. John Stuart Mill B. Herbert Spencer
   C. Jeremy Bentham D. Lester Ward
   E. Auguste Comte

22. Striving to make an athletic team is an example of _____ adaptation.

   A. competitive B. static C. physical
   D. fraternal E. collegiate

23. A race is a major grouping of interrelated people possessing a distinctive combination of physical traits which are the result of

    A. environment   B. skin pigment   C. climate
    D. heredity   E. cultural traits

24. Mobility and interbreeding have produced the phenomenon known as *overlap* and have resulted in the condition that mankind is largely composed of _____ races.

    A. biped   B. hybrid
    C. cross-bred   D. confused
    E. inferior and superior

25. Apart from the several minor races, the three MAJOR races, though they are neither the original ones nor the final or ultimate ones, are Caucasoid, Negroid, and

    A. White   B. Asiatic   C. Oriental
    D. Mongoloid   E. Albino

26. Four factors are responsible for racial differentiation. They are: (1) gene mutation, (2) natural selection, (3) population mixture, and (4)

    A. migration and new races   B. genetic drift
    C. interbreeding   D. skin color
    E. albinism

27. The heavy concentrations of pigment cells in most equatorial populations is a product of natural selection. Pigmentation has, therefore, established itself in hot climates because

    A. of its nutritional value
    B. it is necessary for survival
    C. it is far more comfortable
    D. a hotter climate necessitates darker skin pigment
    E. the equatorial line produces change in any individual

28. The movement of Puerto Ricans to the continental U.S. is an example of

    A. integration   B. status seeking
    C. mongrelization   D. racism
    E. internal migration

29. About half of the Black population lived in urban areas in

    A. 1900   B. 1950   C. 1870   D. 1929   E. 1890

30. The biological concept of ecology deals with

    A. the study of economics
    B. marginal existence
    C. nuances in basic vocabulary
    D. the relationships between organisms and species
    E. thrift and savings

31. In a neolocal family, the married couple lives

    A. at or near an institution of higher learning
    B. in a small town
    C. apart

D. with relatives of the wife's family
E. with the husband's family

32. Fundamental incompatibility of roles is a BASIC cause of
    A. family breakdown
    B. juvenile delinquency
    C. senility
    D. adult crime
    E. homosexuality

33. _____ is the FIRST classic stage of organization.
    A. The church
    B. The school
    C. Industrialization
    D. The family
    E. Agriculture

34. _____ is a PRIMARY factor accounting for greater mobility in the city.
    A. The subway system
    B. Cooperative apartments
    C. A high crime rate
    D. Migration
    E. The job agency

35. According to the Multiple Nuclei Theory, a city is made up of
    A. high and low-rent areas
    B. concentric zones
    C. many small towns and *neighborhoods*
    D. a variety of racial groups
    E. a variety of economic classes

36. The _____ gave up his civilized home for life in a log cabin, exchanged his civilized clothing for the hunting shirt and moccasin.
    A. Bantu
    B. white hunter
    C. Peace Corpsman
    D. Kamikaze
    E. American frontiersman

37. Democracy, realistically and idealistically, found its leadership in Thomas Jefferson. He disliked _____ and defended agricultural interests against industrial interests.
    A. the frontier
    B. cities
    C. Indians
    D. cattlemen
    E. Blacks

38. An important critic of American life says that in all the spheres where moral considerations are meant to operate, men act as though they were being guided by (or rebelling against) rules and prohibitions enunciated by
    A. clergymen
    B. society
    C. a moral mother
    D. Christ
    E. conscience

39. Professor Clyde Kluckhohn's study of the contemporary American pictures them as
    A. rugged individualists
    B. constantly searching for new vistas
    C. dominated by the ever-present father image
    D. imbued with a strong spirit of non-conformity
    E. possessed by a strong spirit of conformity

40. Roles in society are reciprocal.
    The role of the employer may be said to be _____ to that of the employee.

    A. extraneous B. complementary C. democratic
    D. intolerable E. condescending

41. A normless society is termed

    A. disorganized B. non-denominational
    C. culturally lagging D. anomic
    E. diffused

42. Sanctions are forms of reward or punishment based on conformity or

    A. authoritarianism B. obedience
    C. free enterprise D. non-conformity
    E. rational conduct

43. _____ refers to the existence of numerous well-organized groups and associations, all having the same aims and interests.

    A. Class B. Clique C. Homogeneity
    D. Momism E. Pluralism

44. In the view of Pitirim Sorokin, the United States has passed from the sensate to the _____ phase of social change.

    A. pragmatic B. concentrated C. realistic
    D. ideational E. communicative

45. In an organization where power is _____, many small groups compete for control.

    A. primary
    B. money
    C. fragmented
    D. abused
    E. controlled by large groups

46. According to Max Weber, the PRINCIPAL means through which social change occurs, where a unique leader assumes power, is known as

    A. demagogy B. mutation of mores
    C. dictatorship D. hegemony
    E. charisma

47. The word *normal* is often used in three senses:
    (1) average or model in a statistical sense; (2) conforming to certain pre-established standards, and (3)

    A. a sampling of the population
    B. ability to adjust to social changes
    C. adhering to tradition
    D. mediocre
    E. integrated, in the sense that all the parts are operating in coordination with each other

48. _____ is evaluated sociologically according to its effectiveness in bringing about the desired response, rather than according to the moral value of the cause for which it is used.

    A. Public opinion
    B. Prestige
    C. Power
    D. Pretension
    E. Propaganda

49. _____ denotes a person's position in a group with relation to other members of the group, or the position of a group with reference to other groups in some larger totality.

    A. Standard
    B. Status
    C. Salary
    D. Sodality
    E. Stasis

50. Social stratification is the vertical division of society into

    A. varying causes or sympathies
    B. sampling groups
    C. similar social status levels
    D. different social status levels
    E. horizontal juxtapositions

KEY (CORRECT ANSWERS)

1. C	11. E	21. E	31. E	41. C
2. D	12. D	22. B	32. A	42. D
3. E	13. B	23. D	33. C	43. E
4. B	14. E	24. B	34. D	44. D
5. C	15. B	25. D	35. B	45. C
6. B	16. B	26. B	36. E	46. E
7. B	17. D	27. B	37. B	47. E
8. E	18. A	28. E	38. C	48. E
9. C	19. B	29. B	39. E	49. B
10. B	20. A	30. D	40. B	50. D

HUMAN RELATIONS

TABLE OF CONTENTS

	Page
INTRODUCTION	1
FACTS ABOUT PEOPLE	1
FACTS ABOUT RACE	2
RESPONSIBILITY OF GOVERNMENT	2
HUMAN RELATIONS UNDER STRESS	3
BEHAVIOR IN DISASTER	4
EFFECTS OF DISRUPTION OF LIVING HABITS	4

HUMAN RELATIONS

INTRODUCTION

The success of any enterprise is largely determined by its people: Their individual competences, the values they hold, and the quality of their leadership. This generalization stresses attributes important in business, industry, government, or institutional operations, the lack of which produces, at the least, inefficiency and, at the worst, disruption or even destruction of enterprises.

Disaster and civil defense emergency conditions complicate the effective use of personnel, the attainment of objectives, and the control of the citizenry in the affected areas. Normal interpersonal and intergroup relations tend to deteriorate and individual, group, and community effectiveness is lost.

Most of us recognize that understanding and practicing good human relations is important under normal circumstances, but under ordinary conditions most interpersonal adjustments are made simply, easily, and often unconsciously. They are habituated responses learned, practiced, and found effective during countless repetitions of personal contacts. Effective human relations under emergency conditions, however, may be more difficult and their attainment becomes a serious matter for study and understanding.

The phrase "human relations" includes subject matter almost as broad as the study of mankind itself. Many books have been written on the subject. In this brief chapter we can deal only summarily with a few of the more important concepts involved in relations among human beings.

FACTS ABOUT PEOPLE

It is a truism that people are alike in some ways but different in other ways. Handling human relations situations wisely requires sensitivity to individual differences. Physically some people are short and some tall, some fat and some thin. Some adhere to one religion, some to another, and some to none. One person may never have gone to school while his neighbor may have had six years or more of college. Yet the former may be wealthy and the latter relatively poor. One may be an outcast in his neighborhood, one well liked, and still another socially prominent. The first may be a gentle recluse and the last aggressive and domineering. More than likely each of us in large measure reflects the attitudes of our parents or, if we have grown away from these, of a group of our peers. There can be no doubt that we are products of both our heredity and our environment. The interrelationship of various facets of both determine what we are physically, intellectually, and emotionally.

We must recognize that each of us is an individual. Each has his own physique, level of intelligence, special skills and problems, and his own set of beliefs, and prejudice. The latter may include either fear or contempt of the law. Knowing people and recognizing their differences, their strong points and weaknesses, will make us more effective as we attempt to handle emergency conditions and to achieve a measure of normalcy.

While no simple set of "how to" rules can be formulated which will fit all, or even most, human relations situations, a good general principle to keep in mind is the Golden Rule: "Do unto others as you would that they should do unto you"—to which we might add the corollary: *If you had their individual differences*. Therefore, to apply this principle, you will need to study people, and especially their *differences* to be able to "put yourself in the other person's place."

FACTS ABOUT RACE

The term race has many meanings to many people. To some it simply means a group of people descended from a common ancestry and consisting of persons who have similar *physical characteristics*. It is in this sense that many speak of whites, Indians, or black. Others tend to think of races in terms of *nationalities*, such as Italians, Greeks, or Norwegians, insofar as these names denote people coming from various countries or cultures. When majority and minority groups live side by side, a person who essentially is similar to those of the majority, but who has a trace of the minority group characteristics frequently is grouped with the latter. Even competent anthropologists are not in agreement about what constitutes a race and what distinguishes one race from another. Mingling of human stock has gone on throughout recorded history and relative distinctions based on so-called racial characteristics (such as color of skin, hair, etc.) continue to become more obscure.

It is significant that no basic psychological differences between so-called races have been scientifically established. Superficial differences do exist, tend to become exaggerated, and produce commonly accepted stereotypes. It can, in fact, be reasonably concluded that greater psychological differences exist among people of each race than exist among races.

Superiority of one race over another, long an emotional crutch for the personally inadequate and a rallying cry to international and economic conflict, simply cannot be demonstrated. Like it or not, depending on our personal convictions, it can honestly be said that we are "brothers under the skin."

To be very specific, the "knowledge" we commonly hold about race is really an expression of attitudes that we have come to accept and a product of what we have learned to believe.

Relearning some of one's early conditioning about race or learning to minimize it or compensate for it, is necessary for many people if they are to function effectively in situations involving relations with people of other "races."

RESPONSIBILITY OF GOVERNMENT

For government to serve its purpose fully, it must not only apply the law equally and without favoritism, but it must also provide equal protection and service to all. This position can be accepted as an essential principle of the American creed. Nonetheless, diligent effort must always be applied to make this principle a fact of life to all of our people. Therefore, the law itself must be the rule by which we live and work. There can be no fact of a citizen's makeup—color, religion, or economic or social status—that will change his relative position under the law. Poor man, beggar, merchant or thief, although they may conduct themselves differently and hold different beliefs, are each entitled to a common application of the law. It thus becomes imperative that while on duty the individual officer submerge any of his prejudices and beliefs which are contrary to the law and contrary to the above principle. The most critical factor in producing such professional, objective law enforcement action is that he not bend the law to enforce his own code of conduct or utilize his authority out of spite against those who have antagonized him personally.

The police agency's protection and service must be allocated equally and applied freely to all. The agency serves all of the people and neither the status of an individual citizen nor an officer's attitude toward him should influence the agency's kind or level of service.

This composite result of all our interpersonal and interagency contacts is essentially based on job performance and the competence of the agency and of each employee. This refers not only to specific goals which are attained but also to the method by which they are attained and the conduct of all participating employees. An image of an agency gained through a formal public relations program can at best be of only superficial value if it does not reflect the actual worth of the agency. This, in essence, is the distinction between reputations and character. Reputation based on sound characters has lasting value; reputation otherwise based in transient and of dubious value.

There must be a thorough knowledge of human relations by personnel of all ranks. The practice of sound and understanding human relations is bound to strengthen and deepen the department's public relations and to give it lasting character.

Subordination of the officer's personal biases, prejudices, and beliefs to the policy of the department is essential in the handling of incidents and people. If an officer believes his own position is right, but is contrary to that of the agency, he may properly attempt to persuade his superiors to his point of view. He must recognize, however that so long as the agency policy continues, he must conform to it meticulously.

It is simpler to prescribe and require conformity to regulations and procedures which influence public relations than it is to change a man's basic beliefs. If agency policy is based on human understanding, common sense requires that it not only be understood, but also accepted: hence the importance of personnel training in both human relations and public relations.

HUMAN RELATIONS UNDER STRESS

Although human relations to the stress of emergency conditions will vary, they will tend to follow the pattern which is normal to each individual. Individual adjustment to circumstances is usually rapid and effective. Within his own limitations and capabilities each individual will attempt to "carry on." Most will respond to effective leadership and under such leadership may be expected to perform reasonably well under whatever circumstances arise.

However, if one person "panics" or loses control of himself while in the company of others, there is a tendency for his behavior to communicate itself to those about him. There is, therefore, an immediate need to identify any one who shows signs of such behavior. Two courses are then open. First, the person may simply be isolated. This will avoid the contagious effect. Second, he may be given treatment that may involve the use of sedatives on a doctor's orders; other medical measures; use of a psychiatrist, if circumstances permit; supportive efforts of lay persons who can assist the disturbed person to reorient himself. For example, this may sometimes be accomplished by giving him work to do which occupies his mind and reduces his apprehensions. The person who emotionally seeks a scapegoat may also be a source of serious problems. If he is of a dominating nature, he may quickly rally to his "cause" many others who are seeking emotional release, a sense of self-importance, and group identification. Such measures as isolation and treatment may be necessary to minimize his harmful influence.

It is to be expected that there will be some unusual human reactions in time of civil defense emergency or other major disaster that can be considered quite normal. We may expect that these would be manifested in forms less serious than those which we have been discussing. For example, there may be increased muscular tension and bodily responses, and some accompanying psychological manifestations such as excitement and confusion. It is to be stressed, however, that such conditions as a certain stiffness of movement, heavy perspiration, rapid breathing, sudden talkativeness, or unusual quiet are all normal reactions to unusual conditions.

Disaster reactions become abnormal and can be classified as disaster fatigue only when the kinds of conditions indicated above do not pass away quickly and spontaneously without treatment. If a person does not lose or quickly regains his effectiveness, his reaction may be considered normal.

Mild disaster fatigue normally will soon pass without treatment and with no ill effects. It is not usually a concern to emergency personnel except as it somewhat reduces a person's effectiveness. However, if it does not disappear or becomes slightly more severe, we may classify it as moderate disaster fatigue. If the fatigue does not pass or if it tends to become progressively more severe, treatment is indicated and persons so affected should have medical attention. In the case of severe fatigue, medical attention is mandatory. Unless medical service is promptly available, the person may be past susceptibility to treatment and quick recovery. Immediate medical treatment may return persons to normal, prevent increased fatigue and loss of effectiveness, and avoid unusual problems of prolonged care and treatment.

BEHAVIOR IN DISASTER

Concern of civil authorities with people extends, in time, from the normal conditions before disaster to the relatively stable conditions finally achieved after the disaster, whether or not they, in fact, resemble the normal predisaster conditions. It is important to remember that it is during the predisaster normal conditions people must be prepared for disaster. This includes preparing individuals to anticipate disaster conditions, and to accept group organization and training to minimize its effects.

In adequate indoctrination and training have been provided, the warning phase should pose no special problems, but should be a period in which official disaster plans can be placed in effect with individuals taking predetermined precautions, or proceeding to designated posts. Emergency personnel should be on the alert for signs of panic or other disturbances, and be prepared to take appropriate actions.

The impact phase is a critical one because of its disruption of the community and its normal activities. Power may be lost, transportation may break down, and entire geographic areas may be physically isolated or destroyed. This period will be a serious test of plans, organization, uncertainty, and confusion. Persons will have disaster fatigue in all of its manifestations and degrees. Big problems will demand attention and action. As the postimpact phase is entered, recovering from the effects of the disaster will move toward the resumption of normalcy. At this point, special attention must be given to problems of disaster fatigue, prompt treatment provided for those in need, and accommodations provided for those who may require extended care. Many who survive the critical emergency period may now have delayed emotional reactions, and attention must be given to identifying these people and providing them with necessary care.

EFFECTS OF DISRUPTION OF LIVING HABITS

Living in a shelter or relocation area will be an experience with which the average person can draw no comparison from his experience. Unless he has been in military service, or in prison, it will probably be his first experience as an adult in living closely with others not of his own choice. Under these circumstances he cannot simply "be himself." There must be provided effective patterns of group living and he must learn to adjust to them. He will remain an individual, but he must accept a unique responsibility for self-subordination to group goals and conduct. It must be recognized that this, for many, will be difficult, and it must be given due weight by leaders and their staff to induce harmonious, cooperative, and productive patterns of group living.

A special problem will be the presence of many persons separated from members of their families. Sometimes this will be the heartbreaking and final separation of death, and at other times perhaps even more emotion-laden situation of uncertainty about loved ones. Every effort must be made to keep together, or to reunite, members of families.

Other problems will be created by the presence, in some cases, of criminals, drug addicts, and other deviates. The exigencies of group living may well result in magnification of problems of "normal people which are more manageable in normal living. For example, tobacco smokers will need to be controlled for the welfare of all of the inhabitant of a shelter. Habitual smokers deprived of their regular gratification, whether because of shelter rules or because their supply of tobacco is exhausted, will experience discomfort or hardship, and may be irritable. Sexual advances may take place which would not be likely in the same group of people if they were gathered together under more normal circumstances.

Most persons, in establishing their own patterns of living seek harmonious relationships. This often means that people group themselves in communities where there are common backgrounds of race, nationality, religion, education, and employment. Living under emergency conditions, will seldom allow this. People who do not know or "understand" each other will find themselves living closely together under conditions of privation and hardship. In such circumstances, adjustment may be difficult.

In an emergency, there is enforced restriction or mobility. People cannot get away from others whom they would not normally choose as companions. Again, for this reason, everyone must accept unusual responsibilities for harmonious and cooperative living, and leaders must make every effort to minimize frictions imposed by the lack of mobility.

For all practical purposes, normal pursuits will not be available to more than a few. Leaders must seek out opportunities to keep people productively occupied both as individuals and as groups.

The above considerations suggest that leaders and their staff, including law enforcement personnel, will need to be capable of diagnosing and managing human relations situations within the group. Fortunately, research in human behavior provides much in the way of guidelines for such an endeavor, and Federal DCPA courses afford opportunities for leaders and their staffs to increase their capabilities in such matters.

In spite of all of the problems, leaders must keep living conditions as bearable as possible. Since no single way of living will be normal for anyone, the problems of personal adjustment and group leadership will be difficult. Accordingly, leaders have to be on the alert constantly to anticipate difficulties of interpersonal and intergroup relations in time to take preventive action. Avoidance of group tensions and conflict is by far the better course of action than attempts to correct or overcome problem situations once they have developed.

It is a first responsibility of leadership to give confidence to those in the group. While this confidence may sometimes result from an outstanding "natural leader," it is more often the result of a studied effort to build it. The people must be kept as well informed as possible about what is going on in the disaster area.

Leaders must organize and direct activities which may be productive or divertive in nature, but must be meaningful to those who participate. Leaders must be honest about problems, positive in their actions, and impartial and humane in carrying out their decisions. The kind of leadership exerted will largely determine community morale and smoothness of the transition back to more nearly normal living.

6

BRIEF GLOSSARY OF ANTHROPOLOGICAL TERMS

ADAPTATION: The modification of organization in response to selective pressure.

AFFINE: A kinsman by marriage.

AGNATE: A cognatic kinsman to whom ego traces connection through males only.

ANALOGOUS ORGANS: Organs which correspond in general structure, and in function, but not in origin (i.e., they are not modifications of an organ possessed by a common ancestor) Example: the wing of a bird and the wing of a bee are analogous.

CASTE: An endogamous corporate group, membership in which is ascribed by birth, occupying a position in a hierarchy which includes at least one other such group.

CHURCH: A society whose members are united by the fact that they think in the same way in regard to the sacred world and its relation with the profane world, and by the fact that they translate these common ideas into common practices

COGNATE: A kinsman with whom ego shares a common ancester; a consanguineal kinsmen.

CONGREGATION: An aggregate of individuals who regard their collective well being to be dependant upon a common body of ritual performances.

CULTURE: whole which includes knowledge, belief, art, morals, law, custom, and any other capabilities and habits acquired by man as a member of society.

DESCENT RULES: Rules which stipulate the descent line or lines which is or are significant for assigning membership in groups, to individuals.

UNILINEAL RULE: An individual acquires membership in a group from a parent of a stipulated sex. Unilineal rules may be Patrilineal, in which an individual acquires membership in a group from his or her father; Matrilineal, in which an individual acquires membership in a group from his or her mother; or Double Descent, in which an individual acquires membership in Two groups, one through his or her father, the other through his or her mother.

NON-UNILINEAL RULE: Possible membership in the group is defined by descent from a common ancestor to whom an individual may be connected through either males or females or both.

ECOSYSTEM: The total of living organisms and non-living substances which are found within some demarcated portion of the earth's surface, and which are bound together by material exchanges among, the organisms and between tne organisms and the non-living components of the system.

ENVIRONMENT, COGNIZED: The environment as it is understood by those living in it. It is composed of both the material phenomena which the actors know to be present and the non-empirical entities (such as ghosts) which they believe to be present.

ENVIRONMENT, IMMEDIATE: The bounded portion of the biosphere within which an organism or an aggregate of organisms derives it subsistence.

ENVIRONMENT, NON-IMMEDIATE: Those entities existing outside of the bounded portion of the biosphere within which an organism or aggregate of organisms derives its subsistence, but with which it interacts in various ways.

ENVIRONMENT, OPERATIONAL: The environment composed of those material phenomena which an observer discovers to be present and to impinge upon a subject.

FAMILY: An enduring socially approved association which includes at least one pair of sexually cohabiting adults of opposite sexes together with their immature offspring.

FAMILY, CONSANGUINEAL: An association composed of two or more conjugal families bound together by the presence in each of at least one individual who is a cognate of at least one individual in each of the others.

FAMILY, CONJUGAL: A family based upon marriage ties between one adult of one sex and one or more adults of the opposite sex. Conjugal families may be monogamous (nuclear), polygynous (one husband with two or more wives) or polyandrous (one wife with two or more husbands).

FAMILY, NUCLEAR: An enduring socially approved association which includes a single pair of sexually cohabiting adults of opposite sexes together with their immature offspring.

FISSION: A process whereby two independent groups of coordinate status arise simultaneously from a parental group, which ceases to be a functioning group, and the identity of which is forgotten.

FUSION: A process whereby an autonomous group merges with another of coordinate status to form a new group of the same or higher order.

HOMOLOGOUS ORGANS: Organs which correspond in general structure, and in origin (i.e., they are modifications of an organ possessed by a common ancestor) but not necessarily in function: Example: The wing of a bird and the foreleg of a dog are homologous.

MINORITY: An endogamous non-corporate category of people, membership in which is ascribed by birth, occupying a position in a hierarchy which includes at least one other such category.

KINDRED, BILATERAL: A local group composed of a number of families bound together by both consanguineal and affinal ties.

KINDRED, PERSONAL: All of those cognates whom an individual recognizes to be kinsmen.

POPULATION (ECOLOGICAL): An aggregate of organisms having in common distinctive means for maintaining a set of shared trophic relations with other components of the ecosystem in which they participate.

POPULATION (GENETIC): An aggregate of interbreeding organisms enduring transgenerationally.

RACE: A sub-species grouping the members of which are distinguished from the members of coordinate groupings within the same species by the possession of one or more distinctive hereditary traits.

RELIGION: An organized effort, involving beliefs and practices, directed toward the conservation or assertion of socially agreed upon values or modes of behavior by rendering them sacred or by lending to them supernatural support.

RESIDENCE RULES: Rules which stipulate the kinsmen with or near whom a newly married couple takes up residence. Commonly used terms include:

VIRILOCAL	With or near groom's kin
UXORILOCAL	With or near bride's kin
PATRILOCAL	With or near groom's father and his consanguineal kinsmen
MATRILOCAL	With or near bride's mother and her consanguineal kinsmen
BILOCAL	A choice of living patrilocally or matrilocally
DUOLOCAL	Alternation between patrilocal and matrilocal residence
AVUNCULOCAL	With or near groom's mother's brother
NEOLOCAL	Not significantly near any particular kin.

RITE, RITUAL (RELIGIOUS): A conventional act directed toward the involvement of non-empirical (supernatural) agencies in the affairs of the actor.

SCIENCE: Human Behavior directed toward the discovery of regularities among natural events through explicit procedures, and directed further toward the statement of these regularities in propositions which may be validated or invalidated empirically.

SEGMENTATION: A process whereby a group generates subordinate or coordinate groups from its own members without losing its identity.

SIGN: A perceptible aspect of an event that indicates to an observer the occurrence of other imperceptible aspects of the event.

SOCIETY: An aggregate of organisms whose interactions are regulated by a common set of conventions.

SPECIES: The aggregate of organisms which may freely breed with each other but are biologically impeded from interbreeding with members of other aggregates.

SYMBOL: Anything conventionally used or regarded as standing for something else.

SYSTEM: Any set of entities related to each other in such a way that a change in the state of one will cause a change in the state of at least one other.

TABOO: The sacred proscription of a physically feasible action.

TAXONOMY: A systematic ordering of related phenomena into categories and sub-categories by degree of resemblence. The taxonomies presently in use among biologists differ among themselves in some details, but all are based upon the work of Linnaeus, the eighteenth century Swedish systematist. A widely used system ranks categories in the following descending sequences:

Hierarchical Term	Characteristic Name Suffix for Animal Group
Kingdom	
Phylum	
Class	
Sub-class	
Order	- A
Sub-order	- ii
Infra-order	- iforme
Superfamily	- oidea
Family	- idae
Sub-family	- inae
Genus	None
Species	None
Variety	None

UTERINE KINSMAN: A cognatic kinsman to whom ego traces connections through females only.

———

www.ingramcontent.com/pod-product-compliance
Lightning Source LLC
Chambersburg PA
CBHW082046300426
44117CB00015B/2626